Dick and Jane Learn About Money

Mel Clark

Published by Clear Thinking LLC, 2021.

DICK AND JANE LEARN ABOUT MONEY

First edition. March 19, 2021.

Copyright © 2021 Mel Clark.

ISBN: 978-1393183853

Written by Mel Clark.

Table of Contents

Thanks to my loving wife, Linda, who has gone through much of this journey with me.

Prolog

Once upon a time, there were two thirty-something couples with children who found themselves in debt and without savings. Their long-term financial prospects were bleak.

Dick and Jane Jones were married and both had jobs. Dick was 39. Jane was 34. They had two boys, 4-year-old identical twins, Jacob and John.

Lamar and Sally McCoy had been close friends with Dick and Jane since before their children were born. Lamar and Sally also had two children, Calvin, age 6, and Marie, age 3.

Both families lived paycheck to paycheck and struggled to pay their bills.

At the beginning of our story, the Joneses were in their kitchen. They were spending time companionably together while doing their separate chores.

Part One: Getting Control

Scene 1, Friday, 2/14, Year 1

Dick Jones was sitting at the kitchen table. A laptop was lit up between him and the Valentine's Day bouquet of fragrant red roses in the center of the table.

Looking up from the computer screen, Dick said, "I got an email from the bank. Any idea what it's about?"

Without missing a beat as she chopped vegetables Jane replied, "Well, several bills were scheduled to be paid from the checking account. That's probably it."

"Makes sense," Dick said. "Uh oh."

"What's wrong?"

"It says they covered a bill with our automatic overdraft protection. No, two bills. They charged our credit card $300. What're we gonna do Jane? Credit cards are already killing us.

After slamming her chopping knife on the counter, she said, "I told you to watch your spending. How could you let this happen?"

Scene 2, Friday, 2/14, Year 1

That same evening the McCoy family was gathered in their living room. Sally McCoy was sitting on the couch watching television with Calvin and Marie.

Lamar was reviewing their account balances and transactions on the bank's website. He started fidgeting in the desk chair. Then he released a low moan.

"What's wrong Lamar?" Sally asked.

The small boy at her side whined, "Mom! I can't hear the TV!"

"Hush Calvin. I'm speaking with your Father."

At a higher-than-normal pitch, Lamar said, "There's only $42 in our checking account, Sally. We won't see any more money until my next payday. That's Friday. We don't have enough money for groceries, for Heaven's sake!

Sally was silent for a few seconds. Then she said, "Are there any checks out or bills that have to be paid before next Friday?"

Lamar said, "Your next payday isn't until the Friday after mine. We can't get gas. How much do school lunches cost? Do we have food in the house? What are we going to do?"

Marie, her three-year-old daughter whimpered and followed Sally as she stood up and walked to the desk.

Sally looked over Lamar's shoulder and softly said, "Lamar, you're scaring Marie. Can you pull up the bill pay schedule?"

Lamar moved the mouse several times and the bill pay schedule appeared on the screen. She looked at the dates and said, "We'll be fine, Lamar. We just have to stay home this week. We can pack everybody's lunches until Friday. I'll take a look at the checkbook, just in case. But I'm pretty sure there aren't any outstanding checks."

"We've got to get out of this nightmare!" Lamar said.

Scene 3, Sunday, 2/23, Year 1

Dick scanned the traffic through the windshield of their Nissan Maxima as Jane fiddled with the radio controls. "What kind of show are you looking for, my Love?" he asked.

"I don't know," Jane replied. "I'll know it when I hear it, I guess."

"We want Country music!" said Jacob from the back seat. "Yeah," added John.

Jane touched the radio's scan button again and heard a familiar voice. "Hey. I think it's that Dave Ramsey guy."

"So, what's your combined income?" asked a man with a Southern twang.

"$70,000 a year." a Mid-Western male replied.

"And how much debt did you pay off?"

The voice of a Mid-Western woman said, "A little over $100,000. It took us over three years, but we finally got it all paid off. Now we're working on the mortgage!"

"$100,000 of debt paid off in three years on a combined salary of $70,000 a year. That's impressive! How'd you do it?" asked the Southern twang.

"We moved to a cheaper apartment, sold one of our cars, cut the cord on cable TV..." said the Mid-Western man.

"We stopped going out to eat. We cut each other's hair and we shopped really hard for food and anything else we had to buy," finished the Mid-Western woman.

"Wow!" said the Southern twang. Y'all went all-in on beans and rice and rice and beans, didn't you?"

"Yes." The couple said together.

"Are you ready to scream it out?"

"We're ready."

"Here we go, three, two, one..."

"We're debt freeeeeeee!"

"We're debt freeeeeeee!" "Freeeeeeee!" the twins echoed from the back seat.

Dick glanced at Jane and said, "Another couple turned their lives around. I wish it was us."

"We make as much as that couple does and they had more debt than we do now. If they did it, we can do it too," she replied.

"I don't know," he said, "Was that even real? It's probably just actors. Nobody could pay off $100,000 of debt in three years on an income of $70,000 a year. It just doesn't add up."

Jane suggested, "We should check out Dave Ramsey. See if he's legit."

"Yeah. Let's check him out. I bet there's a ton of scam alerts on him."

Scene 4, Tuesday, 2/25, Year 1

Amidst the clatter of knives and forks on china, a small but insistent voice was heard, "I want milk." it said.

"Say please Marie. If you want something, you say please."

"Please."

"Okay Honey", said Sally. "Calvin, will you please pour some milk for your sister?"

Lamar, holding a fork full of mashed potatoes in the air asked, "Have you ever heard of Dave Ramsey, Sally?"

Sally replied, "Not until Dick and Jane told us about his radio program. But I looked him up online. He wrote a bunch of books and runs something called Financial Peace University."

She turned to her son and said, "Thank you, Calvin. You did a good job."

"That's what we need," Lamar said, "Financial Peace. Too bad you have to go to a university to get it."

"Can I have another piece of chicken, Dad?" Calvin asked.

Lamar held up the serving plate. "Sure, here you go," he said. "Do you want a wing or a leg? That's all that's left."

"I want the leg. Thanks, Dad."

You're welcome, Calvin."

"I don't think it works that way," said Sally. "They seem to run workshops, mostly through local churches. One of his books is called Financial Peace too. I wonder if the library has a copy?"

"I'll stop by the library on my way home from work tomorrow and see," replied Lamar. "Would you pass the green beans, please, Sally?"

Scene 5, Friday, 3/6, Year 1

As usual, The Perfect Lunch restaurant was noisy during the noon hour. Sally and Jane leaned in so they could hear each other.

"I finished that 'Financial Peace' book," Sally said. "Lamar is reading it now."

The conversation was interrupted by crashing and clanging as a server cleared the lunch dishes from their table. Sally thanked the server.

"Dick borrowed a copy of the book from a guy at work. I'm about halfway through it." Jane said as she raised her milky coffee for another sip. "Mmmmm, they make such good coffee here."

Sally laughed and said, "Why do you think I always agree to meet you here for lunch, silly. But seriously, Dave Ramsey's plan makes so much sense. We just have to try it."

Jane sipped her coffee, then spoke softly over her cup, "What if it doesn't work?"

Sally set her cup on the table and looked Jane in the eyes. "What if it does?" she said. "It would be wonderful not to worry about having enough money to buy groceries."

"Yeah. And, it would be great to not fight with Dick about money all the time."

"You'd find something else to fight with him about," Sally said, raising her coffee cup once more.

"Probably," Jane replied. "But at least the fight would be about something new."

"Have you gotten far enough to get the gist of the book?"

Jane leaned forward again and said, "Sure, I've read the plan summary, but how would we even start? Baby Step 1 is to save $1,000 in an Emergency Fund. That's a baby step? Who's he kidding? If I could save $1,000, we wouldn't have this problem. Where would Dick and I get $1,000?"

Their server approached the table carrying a pot of coffee and asked, "Would you like a refill?"

"Yes, please," Jane said.

As the server filled Jane's cup Sally said, "That smells wonderful. I'd like a refill too, please."

They thanked the server, who turned to look after other patrons. Then Sally said, "Yeah. It's a big baby step. But it's got to be done. We have to find the money from somewhere."

"Find the money, ha! As likely to win the lottery."

Sally paused, leaned back in her chair, and sipped her coffee. "They say the way to find the money is to figure out every single thing you're spending money on now," she said. "You write it all down. Keep track of it for a while. Then, study what you've been doing. See what you can do without - where you're screwing up. You find some things you can live without, then use that money to save and pay off debt."

"That sounds like a lot of very boring work," Jane complained.

"Yup. But I think it's the only way out."

"Speaking of boring work," Jane said. "It's time to go back to the office."

"You're right." Sally raised her hand to attract the server's attention and said, "Check please."

Scene 6, Saturday, 3/14, Year 1

Lamar grunted as he made a successful corner shot. The ball bounced back through the brightly lit racquetball court unplayable.

"Nice shot, Lamar. Your game."

"Thanks," Lamar said as he wiped sweat from his brow with the tail of his 'I Heart YMCA tee-shirt'. "Did you read that Financial Peace book yet?"

Dick stooped to pick up the ball with his left hand. As he straightened up, he said, "I finished it Tuesday night. Jane doesn't read much, but she read that; and she insisted I read it too."

Lamar, walked toward the front of the racquetball court and asked, "What did you think? Is it all the girls make it out to be? I'm worried it'll be a dead-end."

Dick stopped. He paused for a moment. Then he looked at Lamar and said, "It makes perfect sense. Everything in it is logical and hard. But it might just be something we can do. Jane is motivated to try and so am I."

Lamar shook his head. "Aren't you worried it won't work?"

"I see it this way," Dick replied. "It'll be hard. It'll be painful – we'll have to do without things that seem like necessities. We might not succeed. But if we fail, we won't be any worse off than we are now. So, we have to try."

"I ... I guess you're right. We have to try." Brightening up, Lamar said. "Speaking of trying ... since we're tied one game each, it's time for you to try (and fail) to win this match."

"Right," Dick said as he entered the server's box. "It's all on the line in game three. Bragging rights until next weekend." Then he tossed the ball in the air and served.

Scene 7, Saturday, 4/9, Year 1

"The kids are in bed and the movie doesn't start for a few more minutes," Sally said.

"Please sit. I want to talk for a bit,"

"Okay," said Lamar as he sat on the couch next to his wife.

Sally reached for her husband's hand and said, "Lamar, you don't know how much I appreciate that you were willing to sell your fishing boat. I know how much you love getting out on the water."

"Well Love, I'm going to miss it. That's for sure." He took her hand in his and leaned back on the couch. "But the cash will help pay down our debt. And now we won't have to buy gasoline for the boat or for maintenance, licenses or insurance. So, our monthly expenses will be lower too. What I hate more than giving up fishing for a while is the stress of not having any money to pay bills. That's just the worst. Besides, you gave up eating out and your Mani/Pedi appointments. I had to do my part too."

"Thank you, Lamar. I love you all the more for going all-in to support setting our finances right."

"It's like Dick said, '... if we fail, we won't be any worse off than we are now. So, we have to try." He turned to Sally and kissed her softly.

Sally picked up the remote, pressed the 'on' button, and said, "I think you'll like this movie."

"I hope so."

Scene 8, Saturday, 4/9, Year 1

Jane stopped her Buick sedan in front of the garage and activated the door opener. As the double-wide door rolled up, Spot, their big Dalmatian raced out from under it.

Jane saw Dick standing in front of one of the shelving units. He waved as she got out of the car and Spot jumped up and wriggled all over in greeting.

"How'd the yard sale go?" Dick asked.

"It was great!" she replied. "I beat Sally. I sold $320 worth of stuff and she only sold $275. I put the money in the Emergency Fund at the bank on the way home. Would you help me get some of this stuff out of the car?"

Dick walked around to the back of the car and said, "I love it. There's no temptation that way. How much is in the Emergency Fund now?"

Jane opened the back door of the sedan and picked up a box. "$714.25. We're a little ahead of Sally and Lamar. They have $695.50."

Dick said, "It's not a race, Jane." Then he started walking into the garage with an armload of clothes on hangers accompanied by Spot and his wildly wagging tail.

Jane followed Dick into the garage carrying the box and said, "Maybe not for you. But it is for me. Sally and I are making a game of it. Whichever one gets to $1,000 first has to buy the other coffee ... oops, I mean has to make the other coffee. Anyway, I'm going to win!"

"Okay. I'd like to see you win. How can I help?" he asked as he opened the door leading into the house.

Jane walked through the open door and said, "Well..."

Scene 9, Sunday, 4/10, Year 1

They had taken this route home from church many times. Lamar didn't need to think about it at all. Still, he was quiet. He felt a pang of regret, and grief.

He braked softly stopping their extended cab Ford F-150 for a red light. At last, he turned to Sally and said, "So the idea is to sell the pickup. We'll use the money to buy an old compact sedan. There should be enough money left over to put some in the Emergency Fund. It'll also reduce our insurance bill and how much we spend on gas. Is that it?"

Sally said, "That's it. I don't know how much money will be left to put in the Fund but it should be at least a couple hundred dollars. Enough to put us over the top anyway. The only thing is Jane might get there before we can sell the truck."

"I wanna see!" the shrill voice of their three-year-old daughter filled the passenger compartment.

"What's going on back there?" asked Lamar.

"I wanna see!" the three-year-old cried again.

"I'm just playing a video game, Dad," Calvin replied. "I'm not bothering Marie."

Sally turned in her seat. After taking in the situation she said, "I know you're not doing anything wrong, Calvin. Your Father and I are trying to have a conversation. Can you help us by letting your sister see the screen of your game while you play?"

"Okay," Calvin replied sullenly, followed by little girl giggles.

The signal light turned green and Lamar eased onto the accelerator. He continued the conversation, "I know you want Jane to make your coffee. I get it. But I think it's more important to reduce our monthly spending. That'll let us pay down the debt faster and hopefully we can start a regular monthly deposit to the Emergency Fund."

"That's the plan," Sally said nodding her head. "Thanks for agreeing to it. I know you love this truck."

Lamar looked wistfully around the cab of the truck. "Yeah," he said. "Remember that when our finances are in good shape. Eventually, I'm going to want another one. Maybe a boat too."

Sally touched his arm and said, "When we get our debts paid off and a regular savings plan going, we'll talk about it. But remember, once we get the debts paid off and we're debt-free – we have to stay that way."

"Okay," Lamar said. "But we can save up to buy them, can't we?"

"Sure," said Sally. "But first, let's concentrate on getting out of debt."

"Right," Lamar replied.

Scene 10, Saturday, 4/25, Year 1

Five-year-old Jacob Jones swooshed down the shiny steel as his twin brother, John, raced up the ladder for his next turn down the slide.

Sally stretched her arms overhead and said, "I love this park in the Spring. The Dogwoods and Pear trees are so beautiful. Bringing the kids here to play together was a wonderful idea, Jane."

Jane took a deep satisfied breath. "It's a nice park. I like it here," she said. "The breeze makes it a little chilly today, but that's what jackets are for." Jane smiled and turned to her friend, "Only $10 more, and I win, Sally. Will you make me a latte?"

Sally hesitated as she watched Calvin give Marie a big push on the swing. The push took Marie higher than ever. "Sure, whatever you want. It looks like you'll probably win," she said as Marie screamed with delight. "I'm short $107 and we're only adding $50 a week."

"Spot, get out of the way!' John shouted. John rushed down the slide and the dog moved to the side just in time to avoid a collision.

With a smile, Jane said, "Our next deposit will put us over the top. $60 will go to the bank the day after tomorrow."

"You don't have it in the bag quite yet, Jane. We might sell the pickup first."

Jane's cell phone rang interrupting the conversation. Sally chuckled at Jane's new ringtone for Dick. She watched as Jane listened to her phone.

Jane pushed her hair back with her fingers. Near tears, she said, "How could you do that, Dick? That's terrible! I can't believe it. What have you done?"

Then she was quiet as she held the phone to her ear. Finally, she said, "I'm coming right over. Don't do anything until I get there."

As Jane put her phone away, Sally asked, "What's the matter? What did Dick do?"

Wincing as if in pain Jane answered, "He had a blowout on the freeway and the tire couldn't be repaired. He said he has to buy two new ones to keep the rotations even. This is gonna cost almost $500. I have to go. I'm meeting Dick at the tire store."

Scene 11, Saturday, 4/25, Year 1

Sally sat down on her living room sofa, turned off the TV, and picked up her cell phone. She selected Jane's number on speed dial and waited.

The call connected and Jane said, "Oh. Hi Sally."

"I'm sorry to bother you right now Jane. But I had to tell you we found a backpack that belongs to one of the twins. I'm not sure which one. We didn't open it."

"Thanks, Sally. It's Jacob's. We ran off in such a hurry he forgot it. He remembered when we were halfway to the tire store though. I was planning to go back to the park and look for it soon."

Sally said, "It's safe. I can give it to you Monday during lunch hour."

"If you don't mind, I'll come by later and pick it up. Jacob will need it for Kindergarten Monday morning."

"Sure, no problem," Sally answered. "How did it go at the tire store?"

Jane hesitated, then said, "We didn't have much choice. We could put the tires on the credit card and pay interest. Or we could take the money out of the Emergency Fund. We talked about doing a little of both, but it just didn't make sense."

"So, what did you do?"

Jane said, "You know how Dick is. Always sensible. Always calm. Anyway, he said it would be ridiculous to put the tires on the credit card. The reason for having an Emergency Fund is to take care of things like this, he said. Troubles like these are just life, he said. An Emergency Fund turns them into an annoyance instead of a crisis, he said. So, of course, we took the money out of the Fund. Looks like you win the bet after all."

"You have to get Jacob's backpack, so come on over," Sally said. "I'll make coffee. You can make me a latte in a week or two; after our Emergency Fund passes $1,000."

Scene 12, Sunday, 8/9, Year 1

"Okay. Take up the slack, Dick." Lamar said from underneath the new used sedan.

As Dick turned the crank, the chains connecting the winch to the engine block tightened and strained. The smell of petroleum fumes wafting from under the hood grew stronger. He locked the crank in place and said, "The winch is secure, Lamar."

Lamar scooted a bit, adjusting his position under the engine compartment. "Thanks," he said. "What were you saying about your Emergency Fund?"

"We finally hit the $1,000 mark. Buying those new tires was a big hit. It set us back more than three months. But we finally did it," Dick said.

Lamar grunted with effort. "Can you hand me that cheater bar?"

Dick picked up the big lever. It cast a sharp shadow in the bright afternoon sunshine. He bent down and extended it under the car so that it touched Lamar's hand.

"Thanks," Lamar said grasping the cheater bar. "Trading my pickup for this old sedan put us over the top and gave us a start on paying off debt too. I miss my truck though."

"Do you regret selling it?"

"No. We had to make room in the budget to pay off the credit cards. But I still miss it." Lamar replied and grunted. "There! It's moving."

"Thank God we had enough money in the Emergency Fund to cover the cost of those tires," Dick said. "If that blowout happened even a few months earlier, we'd have had to pay for them with a credit card. More debt, more interest. We lucked out."

"Seeing what you went through and how well your Emergency Fund worked...well, I'm glad Sally, and you too, talked me into doing this money makeover thing," Lamar said. "My stress level is the lowest it's been in years."

"Even with the stress of putting sweat equity into this old car?"

Lamar grunted again. "There. The thing is finally off. Can you hand me the new one, Dick?'

Dick squatted low to put the new motor mount in Lamar's hand. Lamar pushed it into position and said, "Yup. You know working on cars is not my favorite thing," Lamar said. "But even with fixing up this old sedan, and missing my pickup, my stress level is way lower."

Dick replied, "Mine too. Now it's time for us to focus on paying off credit cards."

"Yeah," said Lamar, "although right now I'm kind of focused on this motor mount. I need the wrench again, Dick. Do you see it?"

"Here it is," Dick said. He moved the wrench so Lamar could see it. "It was behind your shoulder."

Lamar picked up the wrench and started tightening bolts. "Thanks," he said.

Part Two: Getting Out of Debt

Scene 13, Tuesday, 8/11, Year 1

Jane sat quietly on the living room floor. She looked at the multitude of papers in shoeboxes arrayed around her. Then she looked up at her husband who was also sitting on the floor a few feet away. She said, "How many people do we owe money? Do we even know?"

"I'm not sure," Dick replied. "We pay the bills as they come in."

Jane picked up the box labeled for this year and said, "To make the "debt snowball" work we need to know what debts we have. But there's so much."

"Yeah. It's a bit overwhelming. We just have to get it all organized. I printed copies of the bills we got by email over the last six months and a couple of bills that are set to auto-pay." Dick said.

"This year's receipts are in this box. There might be duplicates with what you printed."

Dick said, "It doesn't matter. Let's go through the last several months of bills and make a list of them."

"First," said Jane, "let's make a stack for each month. January goes here. Here's February."

"Here are March and April," Dick said as he started two new piles.

Jane said, "And, this stack is May. Maybe we should, like, spread them out and make a stack for each company?"

"That's a good idea. After we go through these, let's get everything from last year too. I think we pay some quarterly. If I remember right, we only pay personal property taxes once a year."

They sorted through the papers again making a separate stack for each bill. After noticing a pile of credit card bills between the electric company and their family dentist, Dick asked, "Can we move all the credit card and other debt type bills to one side and keep the bills for services, like electricity, cable TV, and medical stuff over here?"

"Sure." Jane agreed and started rearranging the piles.

Just then, their big dog, barking happily, ran through the living room scattering the piles of papers.

"Oh no! Jane shouted. "Spot! Sit!" commanded Dick.

The playful Dalmatian immediately sat on the gas company stack.

Their two five-year-old boys ran into the room catching up with Spot.

"Stop, boys!" Dick said. "Don't move!" said their mother.

The twins collapsed to the floor giggling. "This looks like fun," said one. "Can we help?" asked the other.

"You can really help by taking Spot back to your room and stay there with him until we finish and straighten up in here," Jane said.

"Okay, come on Spot," Jacob said.

The dog looked at the boy and bunched up his muscles preparing to move. But he didn't get up. He looked at Dick expectantly.

Dick made eye contact with the dog for a few seconds. Then he said, "Okay, Spot. Good boy."

Spot jumped up and ran after the twins. In seconds a door slammed and calm returned to the living room.

Jane looked at the papers on the floor. "It could have been worse," she said. They began restacking the bills and receipts.

After five minutes of working silently, Jane said, "We have debts from four different credit cards and three student loans. We also have this home equity loan – does that count? It's kind of a mortgage isn't it?"

Dick replied, "It's a mortgage all right. But our mortgage is a debt too. And, we treat the home equity loan like a credit card, drawing money out when we need it."

After another thirty minutes of organizing papers, Jane said, "Finally. That's all of them for this year and last year."

"I hate to say it, Jane, but we're not done yet. We need to go through the email bills from last year to make sure we haven't missed any. Plus, for each company, we need to find the most recent bill so we can write down the name of the bill, the amount, the due date, and the interest rate, at least for the debts."

Jane looked at the piles on the floor with a grimace and said, "I'll find the most recent bills from each company and write the information on a notepad. You search the emails."

"Sounds like a plan," Dick responded. When we're done, I'll put it all in a spreadsheet."

Scene 14, Saturday, 8/15, Year 1

Sally looked up at the bright sun surrounded by a clear blue sky, then over to her daughter playing in the backyard sandbox adjacent to the swing set. She said, "It's a beautiful day to work in the yard, isn't it, Lamar?"

Lamar pushed the shovel with his foot sinking it into the clay soil. He lifted the dirt and tossed it on a growing pile. "Yeah. It's a pretty day." He said slowly. "I'm kind of stuck on what you were saying earlier though. About paying off the smallest credit card first."

"Well, do you want to talk about it while we work?" she asked.

"Yeah. You were saying, if we pay off the smallest card first, we'll have more cash because of the minimum payments. How does that work? he asked.

"Right," Sally answered. "There's a minimum payment due on every credit card. We have to pay at least the minimum on each one every month. If we focus our extra cash on the smallest one, we can pay it off quickly. When we get it paid off, its minimum payment goes away. That will leave more money to use on the next card we focus on."

Lamar didn't respond immediately. He pulled another shovel of dirt from the hole. Then he said, "But why do the minimum payments matter?"

"Minimum payments are a bigger percentage of the balance when the balance is small. So that payment takes money away from the card you're trying to pay off quickly. If you concentrate on the smallest card on purpose, you can use your money more efficiently." she said.

Lamar stopped and leaned on his shovel. After a few seconds, he said, "It sounds a little like hocus pocus. What about the interest rates? Aren't they important?"

Sally said, "Sure. Interest rates are important."

She stopped speaking and put her hand into the hole. "It's deep enough for the bush," she said. "You don't have to dig anymore. Can you pour in a little of that water while I add topsoil?"

Lamar slowly tipped a bucket and water sloshed into the fresh hole. Sally put several handfuls of topsoil in with the water. Then she continued, "Interest rates do matter. But they matter most for the biggest bills. When we get the two smaller cards paid off, we'll have a lot more money available every month to pay on the highest interest rate card."

She looked at the bush from several different angles. Finally, she said, "Can you set it in the hole with this side toward the front?"

Lamar carefully positioned the bush in the hole.

"Thanks," she said. "Turn it clockwise a bit. Yeah. That's good."

Sally got up and walked about fifteen feet in front of the bush. She turned and looked at it. "I don't know, Lamar. Turn it a little more clockwise. Great. That's better. You can start covering it with dirt now."

Lamar carefully spread a shovel of dirt around the bush and said, "It just doesn't feel right paying off the credit card with the lowest interest rate first." Then he stuck the spade in the dirt for another load.

"Paying off the smallest card first has another advantage," Sally said.

"What's that?"

Sally smiled and said, "Endorphins! Just think how good it'll feel when we make that last payment."

"You got that right," Lamar said. "It'll be a rush. Okay, let's do it."

Scene 15, Wednesday, 9/23, Year 1

Jane held the offer letter in both hands and scanned it one more time whispering to herself.

She looked over at Spot. The big Dalmatian was lying quietly in the corner formed by the refrigerator and the kitchen wall.

She said, "Spot, this is too good to be true."

Spot looked up and thumped his brushy tail on the floor several times.

"Right, I know," she said. "If it seems too good to be true, it probably is."

She picked up her cell phone and touched her speed dial for Sally.

After three rings, Sally answered, "Hey, Jane! What's up?"

"I just read an offer we got in the mail today," Jane said. "It seems too good to be true. I wanted to talk to you about it before I mention it to Dick."

Hearing Jane's voice, Spot once again raised his head and wagged his tail thumping it repeatedly on the tile floor.

Jane smiled at their pet and listened as Sally said, "That's worrisome. We need to stick to our plans, Jane."

"I know," Jane replied. "We paid off our smallest credit card this month and we plan to start working on the highest interest rate card next. But maybe this thing that came in the mail can help us. It says if we open a new credit card account and transfer the balance of a current credit card to the new one, they'll give us a zero percent interest rate for eighteen months. What do you think?"

Sally was quiet for a moment. Jane could hear Lamar in the background reading a children's book out loud.

"Opening a new credit card doesn't sound good," Sally said. "I don't think Dave Ramsey would approve." She paused again, then continued, "How much can you transfer and what would the interest rate be after eighteen months are over?"

"It says you can transfer up to $3,000. Let's see, the interest rate will be 14.9% at the end of the period," Jane said.

"That's less than your highest rate card now isn't it?"

"Yeah."

Sally said, "Sometimes they charge big fees for balance transfers. Do you know if this one has a fee?"

"I didn't see one."

"Well, read it over again carefully and look for a fee. I think they usually add it to your credit card balance when they make the transfer," Sally said. She watched the light steady rain through the kitchen window as she waited for Jane to read the fine print.

Jane replied, "Right. Hold on a minute, Sally." She turned the page over and read the back. Then she stopped and said, "You're right Sally. They charge a 3% fee. 3% of the amount transferred is added to the balance. Still, that's a lot less than the 18.9% they would tack on if we leave the balance where it is now."

Sally said, "It's a little scary, but it does seem worth investigating. Let's check it out on Clark Howard's website, clark.com. He may know about some even better balance transfer offers. Can you pull his website up on your computer?"

Jane responded, "I just pushed 'enter'."

Scene 16, Saturday, 10/10, Year 1

"Ouch! That quarterback took a hit!" Lamar said.

"At least he can recover in the locker room for a while. That's a tough way to end the half though." Dick muted the television for half-time. "The Tigers are only down by seven," he said.

"Yeah, they'll come back," Lamar said as he reached for a handful of pretzels.

Dick leaned back on the couch and sipped his beer. "How many kids are coming to Marie's birthday party?" he asked.

"Seven," Lamar answered. "Three boys and four girls. All of them from Marie's pre-school class."

Dick said, "It's good that we managed to get out of the party preparations. I really wanted to watch football today."

"Honestly, I think the girls wanted us out of the way," Lamar said. "They were happy to get rid of us for the afternoon. As long as we're back before the party starts at 5:30."

"When she said, 'Shoo, go find something to do.' Sally wasn't all that subtle," Dick said.

Lamar laughed. "I was happy to comply. It's great we could see the game from your house while they get ready for the party at my house."

"I agree."

Lamar took a pull from his beer and said, "I can't believe the deal the girls found on Clark Howard. Moving $10,000 to the new credit card interest-free is a game-changer." Then he crunched into a pretzel.

"It sure is," Dick replied. "Even after the 15-month zero-interest promotion ends, the rate is lower than we're paying now. We just have to be sure we don't buy anything with that zero-interest card until the 15-month promotion is over."

"We're going to put the new card away in a drawer until it's safe. Of course, we're not using credit cards at all anymore. Dave Ramsey doesn't like them," Lamar said as he bit into another pretzel.

Dick said, "We still use our lowest rate card for convenience. But when we make a payment on it, we pay the total of the new charges, plus the interest. Of course, we would make the minimum payment if it were higher. So, the effect is like we didn't use the card at all."

Lamar said, "That takes a lot of discipline. I think we're better off doing it the Dave Ramsey way."

Dick reached into the pretzel bowl.

"How do you work paying off the high-interest rate cards?" Lamar asked, then sipped his beer.

"Except for the way we use the lowest rate card, we do things about the same as you and Sally," Dick said. "We only have balances left on three cards. One of them is the lowest rate card that I already talked about. We make the minimum payment on the second-highest rate card. And, we put as much money as we can against the highest rate card."

"Are you actually going to use your home equity loan to pay off a credit card? Lamar asked. That sounds dangerous to me."

Dick chewed for a few seconds. Then he said, "It does feel a little risky. But we're committed to getting completely out of debt. This will help. Instead of 13.9% we only pay 4% on the home equity line. But we're not going to get the card completely paid off that way. We're borrowing $15,000 from the home equity line and applying it to our highest rate card. After that, we'll be able to pay off the card in about five more months.

Lamar took another sip of beer and said, "Still seems scary. I'm glad Sally and I don't have a home equity loan. That's not an option for us. Hey, turn the volume back on Dick. They're showing highlights of the Baylor game."

Scene 17, Thursday, 10/15, Year 1

Lamar pulled the sedan into a convenient parking space near the door. The cinnamon spice air freshener hanging from the rear-view mirror swayed back and forth. He turned off the ignition. Then he put his hands back on the wheel at ten and two. He said, "Well, we're here. I don't like this Sally. The idea of taking out a home equity line makes me nervous. And we're taking time off work to do it too."

Sally remained in her seat and said, "I know and I'm sorry, Lamar. But it just makes sense. Look how well it's working out for Dick and Jane."

Lamar reluctantly released his grip on the steering wheel. He turned to his wife and said, "Yeah, but it's a second mortgage on our house."

"We don't have to do anything today," Sally said. "Let's at least talk to them and find out what our options are. We may not even qualify."

"Okay. But I don't like it. The sky is dark and overcast and that's just the way I feel."

They got out and met in front of their car. Sally took Lamar's hand and they walked through the door of the Hometown Federal Bank.

Scene 18, Thursday, 10/15, Year 1

Sally looked at the mortgage loan officer across the big maple desk. She smiled and said, "That all sounds good, David. But can you summarize the benefits for us?"

The loan officer returned her smile and said, "Sure. So, here's how it works out." He turned a yellow legal pad sideways so all three of them could read it. "If you refinance your existing mortgage for 30 years at this rate," he said as he circled the interest rate with his pen, "and roll the fee into the principal balance," he underlined a number on the pad, "your monthly payments will be $250 per month less than they are now."

He paused and looked up at Sally. "Then, since you'll have more than 20% equity, you can also take out a home equity line later if you want."

Sunlight started streaming through the window to his left as Lamar leaned forward in his chair. "I like that option a lot better," he said. "We won't have a home equity line. We'll just have one mortgage and an extra $250 per month to pay down other debt."

Sally looked at Lamar. Then she turned back to the loan officer and said, "When we get rid of all the other debt, can we start paying off the mortgage early too? That's not a problem is it?"

The loan officer flipped over some of the pages on his desk. He pointed to a clause in the mortgage application. "No. Of course not," he said. "It says right here in the contract that there are no prepayment penalties for paying off this mortgage early."

"Can we make double payments with all of the extra going against principle?" asked Lamar.

"No problem."

Sally and Lamar turned to each other. Sally asked, "Well, what do you think, Lamar? Should we do it?"

"Absolutely!" Lamar said with a big grin.

The loan officer said, "We can get started by filling out these forms..."

Scene 19, Saturday, 1/16, Year 2

"It's so cold out," Jane said. "This hot coffee is just what I need to warm me up."

Sally replied, "Yeah. At least it's not snowing."

"Wow! What a shot!" Lamar's voice drifted in from the living room.

Jane said, "It didn't take long for the boys to get involved in that basketball game."

"No. They're totally absorbed," Sally said. She broke her chocolate chip muffin in half and took a bite.

"I can't believe your company is going out of business, Sally. After 75 years!" Jane said as she spread butter on half of her muffin.

"It's a shock losing my job like that," Sally said. "The company closes its doors on February 3rd."

"Do you mind if I pop this in the microwave to melt the butter?" Jane asked.

"Here, let me," Sally replied. She took the plate from Jane's hand and set the microwave for thirty seconds. When the timer dinged, she retrieved the muffin for Jane and sat down.

"What will you do Sally?" asked Jane. She bit into the warm muffin lavished with butter.

"I'll find another job of course," Sally said. "Hopefully with a company that's better managed." She sipped her coffee. Then she said, "They've been going downhill for years. I guess it was inevitable. I wish they could've found someone competent to lead them. But, It's too late now."

Jane asked, "Will you be okay financially?"

"Since we started on this money makeover thing, Lamar and I have eliminated a lot of debt. And we've cut our expenses enough that we can get by on just his salary for a while," Sally answered. "We won't be able to make any progress on paying off debt though. Not until I find another job."

Sally continued, "Our emergency fund will bridge the gap until my unemployment benefit kicks in. I think that'll be a week or two after the company closes. Or maybe after I get my last paycheck, I'm not sure about that."

She took a bite of her muffin and a sip of coffee. After a few seconds, she added, "I hate to admit it, but Lamar was right about the home equity line. I'm glad we don't have one of those now.".

Jane put her coffee cup back on the table. "Are you just going to make minimum payments on your credit cards until you find another job?" she asked.

"Yup. And minimum payments on the credit cards are less than the home equity loan minimum would be," Sally said. "That's why I'm glad we didn't do it."

"That's worrisome. Our home equity loan is maxed out."

Sally said, "You'll be okay. Your job is pretty safe, isn't it? And Dick's too?"

Jane hesitated, holding her muffin in her hand. Then she said, "They seem to be. But I'll feel better when we get the debts paid off."

"You and me both," Sally answered.

Suddenly, all four children ran up the stairs and into the kitchen with Calvin in the lead.

"We want muffins too!" Calvin shouted. "Muffin!" said Marie.

Sally laughed and said, "Quiet down and go wash your hands. All of you. There'll be muffins for you when you settle down and clean up. Now go!"

Scene 20, Saturday. 4/17, Year 2

Lamar tossed a ball in the air and caught it as they walked down the hallway toward the racquetball court. "We really should do this more often, Dick. It's cheap, it's exercise, and it's more fun than walking on a treadmill," he said.

"All true," said Dick. "Have you thought about joining the league they're starting next month?"

"I didn't even know about it."

Dick stopped and pointed. "There's a flyer about it on that bulletin board."

They stopped to read the flyer. Lamar said, "That's interesting. But it isn't covered by our YMCA dues. It costs an extra $25. I don't think that's a good idea right now. I'll talk to Sally about it this evening."

"Maybe you can qualify for a senior discount now that you're a year older."

"Turd!" Lamar said. "Forty-one doesn't qualify as a senior anything."

Dick turned to Lamar and asked, "How's Sally's job search going?"

"I'm worried about her," Lamar said. "It's been three months and she still hasn't found a job. I think she's getting depressed."

"How are you holding up?"

"I'm okay. We tightened our belts a little more. Cheaper food. Less driving. We finally cut the cord on cable TV. So, we're getting all of our bills paid. We're better off than we were last year. But Sally needs to work. She needs it for her sense of worth and so we can finish paying off the debt."

They resumed walking.

"How's it working out with child care expenses? Dick asked.

"Sally staying home does save a lot on child care," Lamar said. "It was costing us about a third of her salary, so it definitely helps. The kids sure like having her around too."

"Did she file for Unemployment Compensation?"

"Yeah, she's getting Unemployment, but we're putting most of it in the Emergency Fund. It runs out in three more months, so we're trying to live without it. So far, it's working. We don't want to be dependent on Unemployment checks and have them stop before Sally finds another job"

Dick slowly pushed open the door of the court. Fumes from a recently used cleaning agent assaulted their nostrils. After checking to make sure the court was empty, they entered.

"Has Sally thought about freelancing?" Dick asked. "Her skills ought to be marketable that way."

They walked to the center of the court and Lamar said, "We're talking about it. She found some web sites and apps where she might be able to get gigs. It just seems so risky."

"Riskier than being unemployed?"

"Well... I guess not." Lamar said. "Who's going to serve first?"

Dick replied, "Spin the racquet, and let's find out."

Scene 21, Saturday, 5/22, Year 2

Sally and Jane walked down the department store aisle. They stopped at a display table in the brightly lit Boys Department. Jane rifled through a stack of green t-shirts looking at the size tags.

"Do you always buy two of everything? Sally asked.

"No. Only about half of the time, I guess," Jane said. "Even though they're twins they each have their own personalities and tastes."

"But you're buying two of those blue shirts and two of the red ones."

"They have differences," Jane said. "But they also have a lot in common. Often, they want to dress alike – just to mess with people, I think. Ah. Here's a pair of green ones in their size."

Sally moved to the next display and picked up a blue and white striped shirt. "I think this will look good on Calvin," she said.

Jane put the green t-shirts in her basket then she asked, "How was your first gig, Sally?"

Sally checked the size of the blue and white shirt, then she put it back on the table. "It was a start. But it didn't pay much," she said. "It took a lot of time to get organized and figure out how to work from home. I would have made much more money working at McDonald's. But I learned a lot. Next time will be better."

Jane said, "I kind of envy you, getting to work from home."

Sally flipped through more shirts on the table. She picked up another blue and white one. "Don't envy me yet. It's gonna be a while before I make enough money to make the whole thing worthwhile. If I ever do," she said.

After confirming the size, Sally put the blue and white shirt in her basket. Then she said, "The thing is, I can't do it halfway. I either go all in and make it work or I have to put my energy back into finding a job."

As they wandered over to the jeans section, Jane said, "Dick told me you're doing okay on just Lamar's salary. Doesn't that take the pressure off?"

Sally answered, "Like you, we cut our expenses a lot over the past year. That makes it possible for us to live on just Lamar's salary. And it is working out. I still feel the pressure though. I want to finish what we started – pay off the rest of our debt. I want to save for retirement and for the kids' educations. If I can make enough money to put us back on that track, I'll call it a success. Then you can envy me."

"I look forward to it," Jane said. "Are you ready to check out?"

"Yeah. Let's go. I want to take a look at the new store that opened last month."

"The one on Guilford Road?" Jane asked. "It looks expensive."

"That's the one. I don't want to buy anything. I just want to see what they have."

"Sure, that'll be fun."

Scene 22, Monday, 11/8, Year 2

Jacob and John looked at each other, then at their food. Simultaneously, they stuck their forks into bits of pork chop and slowly raised them to their mouths. They hesitated. As one, they popped the bits into their mouths and broke out laughing.

"Oh my!' said Jane. "What will they come up with next?"

"They're going to be an awesome team by the time they're in high school," Dick said. "It'll be a sight to behold."

You're right, Dick. But will they be a force for good?" Jane asked.

"Of course, they will. They're good kids. And it's our job to make sure they stay that way."

"A daunting challenge," Jane said. "On another subject, Sally finally did it."

Dick finished his sip of water and set the glass down behind his plate. "What'd she do?" he asked.

John slipped his hand down below the table and gave a cheese-covered broccoli sprout to the eagerly waiting Spot.

Jane said, "Please pass me the bread, Jacob." Then she turned to her husband. "She made enough money freelancing that they paid off more debt last month than they did the month before she lost her job."

Jacob handed the bread plate to Dick who passed it to Jane. "That's fantastic! I'm so happy for them," Dick said.

"Yeah... it's great." She replied. "I wish I could work from home too." Finally noticing John's sneaking behavior, she said, "We don't feed the dog at the table, John. It teaches him bad habits."

"Spot. Go lie down," commanded Dick.

Spot trotted out of the kitchen.

Part Three: Planning for the Future

Scene 23, Thursday, 4/7, Year 3

Dick smiled as his fingers danced on the keyboard of his laptop computer. He stopped for a moment and sat up straight in the kitchen chair resting his hands on the table.

Jane, standing a few feet away, opened the cabinet door and carefully placed another dinner plate on the growing stack. She glanced at the digital clock on the face of the microwave. Then she called through the kitchen doorway, "Boys. It's 8:30. Start getting ready for bed. Whose turn is it to shower first tonight?"

A disembodied voice answered, "It's John's turn. I showered first last night."

"Alright," Jane said. "Go take your shower, John."

"Aw, Mom."

"Go."

Spot walked into the kitchen. He sat in his favorite place, beside the refrigerator, and looked at the couple.

Dick leaned forward and triumphantly hit the enter key on his laptop. He looked up at Jane and said, "That's it, Jane. We've made the last payment on the last student loan. Only the mortgage is left."

Jane stopped. She sat down beside Dick at the kitchen table and said, "Wow! What a relief!

I never thought we'd do it. When is the party?"

Dick got up and poured a cup of coffee from a freshly made pot. "Do you want some coffee, Jane? It's decafe," he said.

"That's not what I had in mind for a party, but yes, I'll have a cup," she answered.

Dick poured coffee into a second cup, added cream and sugar, and set it in front of Jane. As he sat back down beside his wife, he said, "It's too soon to party. I think... I think we should save more for our retirement."

Jane looked up wide-eyed. "I thought the plan was to double up on mortgage payments," she said. "Get completely debt-free, so we could scream it out on Dave Ramsey's radio show." Then she sipped her coffee.

Spot stood up, walked around in circles, and finally curled up in the corner against the kitchen wall and the refrigerator.

Dick brought the still-steaming coffee to his lips. When he set it down, he said, "Yes, that's what we agreed to do last year. But now I think we need to focus on saving for retirement. It's starting to get real for me. Our parents never got around to it. I don't want us to be like them."

Jane chuckled. Then she said, "We're already not like them. We're out of debt. We're even putting money in 401k plans at work."

Dick looked thoughtful. Then he said, "That's true. But it's not enough. We can do better now."

Jane sipped her coffee. Then she put the cup down. "Paying off the mortgage early is doing better," she said.

"What if we split the difference? Dick asked. "We could put half of the debt payment money against our mortgage. We'd still pay it off early. Then we could put the other half into retirement accounts. How about that?"

"Let me digest it for a while," Jane replied.

Dick said, "Sure. We can talk about it tomorrow." Then he started shutting down his computer.

Scene 24, Saturday, 7/16, Year 3

"Let's go for a walk Lamar," Sally said, rising from the plush living room armchair.

Lamar looked down at Calvin and Marie lying on the floor watching the television. Then he looked up at Sally and said, "Marie will be all pumped up when we get back. It'll make it hard to get her to bed on time."

Sally said, "I mean just the two of us. Calvin is 9 years old. He can watch his sister for half an hour. Can't you Calvin?"

Lamar said, "Do you think so?"

Calvin chimed in, "Sure. We'll be fine, Dad. Besides, I don't wanna go on a walk. I wanna see the rest of this show."

"Come on Lamar," Sally said. "Let's go before someone changes their mind,"

Lamar stood and followed his wife to the front door. He turned and said, "You two stay put. We'll just be walking around the block. We'll be back in a few minutes."

"Bye Dad!" Calvin and Marie said together.

Lamar and Sally walked out the front door of their house and turned right onto the sidewalk. Then Lamar took Sally's hand and they strolled quietly for a while.

Lamar said. "It's still a little warm this evening. But at least it's not blistering hot like it was at 2 o'clock."

"Yeah, it's a nice evening for July," Sally said.

They continued walking quietly for a few minutes. Then Lamar asked, "What's on your mind, Sally?" This is out of character for you."

"What? Can't we go for a walk once in a while?" Sally asked.

"Sure," Lamar replied. "But you seem worried."

Sally hesitated. Then she said, "I'm not worried exactly, but I've been thinking about something."

"Uh oh. What plot are you hatching now?

"My freelancing business is doing better than I ever expected," she said. "Last month I cleared more money than I used to take home from my old job."

Lamar said, "Your business is putting us over the top. We're gonna pay off the last of our debts in about six months – except for the mortgage, of course. We're making more money and our expenses are lower. We're doing really well, Sally."

Sally didn't say anything as they turned the corner of their block and continued walking.

Finally, she said, "You know, Dick and Jane started Roth IRAs last month,"

"Yeah, I heard, Lamar said. "They're ahead of us. They've already paid off their debts. And they're making extra mortgage payments too."

Sally said, "They're more ahead of us than that. Since I lost my job, I couldn't contribute to my 401k anymore. I'm not allowed to."

Lamar stopped walking. He gently pulled Sally to a stop beside him. Then he turned to her and said, "You aren't thinking about investing instead of paying off the debt, are you? I don't like that idea. It's scary."

Sally looked him in the eye and said, "Nothing so drastic. I'm thinking that if my business continues to grow, any extra could go toward retirement. Maybe I could open a Roth IRA too."

Lamar hesitated a few seconds. Then he said, "So, we'd still get the debts paid off in six months?"

"Sure. I want that too. But I also want to start saving for retirement again."

"I'm good with that," Lamar said. Then he took Sally's hand again and they continued their walk.

Scene 25, Sunday, 7/17, Year 3

Dick lifted his cup from the kitchen table. He sipped steaming coffee and looked at the computer screen. "Huh," he grunted softly.

"Is something wrong?" Jane asked. She put the leftover green beans on the countertop and turned to her husband. "Things have been going so well. I knew it couldn't last," she said.

Dick replied. "Relax. Nothing's wrong. We just maxed out our Roth IRAs for the year. We're not allowed to make another contribution until January."

"Oh," Jane said. "What do we do with the money now? Is it time to party yet?"

"No parties," Dick said. "I've been thinking about the answer to your other question though. We can increase our 401k contributions for the rest of the year.

"You mean just temporarily, right? I like the Roth IRA. I like the idea of never having to pay taxes on the money after you put it in the account. I want to max it out every year."

"I agree. We should max them out every year. The question is, what do we do for the rest of this year?"

Jane said, "Okay then, what do we do?" She sat down across from Dick. Spot, sensing an opportunity, trotted over to her chair and sat beside her.

"At the rate we're currently contributing to our 401k plans, we'll only get to about 30% of what we're allowed. We can put the Roth money in our 401k's. We can do that and still be well below the 401k limit at the end of the year."

Jane rubbed Spot's head and neck and the dog leaned against her knee. "But what about maxing out the Roths next year?"

"At the end of the year, we'll have to do the arithmetic again," Dick said. "In January, we can start putting money into the Roths every month again. The goal would be to max it out in December. Under the current rules, we can each contribute only $6,000 per year. So, we can put $500 a month in each of our accounts. That gets us both to the $6,000 limit in December."

"And the rest will go to our 401k's?" Jane asked.

"Right. Our 401k contribution next year will be higher than it's been up to now. But from now until the end of the year it'll temporarily be even higher."

"What if we get a raise?" asked Jane.

"That would be a good problem. We'll figure it out when it happens," Dick said. "It's also likely that at some point the laws will change. Eventually, they'll probably increase the Roth contribution limit. We'll just have to tweak it when things change. You can remind me to check it once in a while."

"I definitely will!" Jane said. "Hey! Do you hear that?"

Dick hesitated for a moment. Then he said, "I don't hear anything."

"That's the sound of silence. You better go see what mischief the twins are getting into."

Dick smiled and said, "Right. I'm on my way."

Scene 26, Saturday, 1/28, Year 4

Lamar rested the tray of nuts and cheese on the coffee table and sat on the couch beside his wife.

Sally reached forward and selected a cube of swiss cheese.

Leaning back on the couch, Lamar slowly shook his head. "I can't believe we did it," he said. "Except for the mortgage, we're out of debt.":

"Feels good, doesn't it?" Sally said.

"It's amazing! It's been three long years, but we made it."

Sally turned and set her drink on the end table. Then she said, "Now we have to decide where to put our extra money next."

Immediately, Lamar replied "We have to pay off the mortgage. Someday, I could lose my job, like you did. I don't want to have to scramble to find a way to pay the mortgage. Without the mortgage payment, we could live on your business for however long it takes me to find another job."

Lamar pulled out a handful of mixed nuts from the bowl in the center of the tray.

Sally picked up her tea and blew softly across the surface. Then she said, "Yeah. But really, your part is easy."

Lamar swallowed. "I don't understand. What's the difference?"

"You're contributing to your 401k and the rest of your money goes to increase the mortgage payment," Sally said. "I don't have that option."

"Why not?" Lamar asked. "I mean, I know you don't have a 401k anymore, but you're paying into your IRA and putting the rest against the mortgage – just like me. So how is it different?"

"I guess you haven't noticed, but I'm getting kind of stressed," Sally said. "My freelancing business is doing well. I keep taking more clients and working more hours. I'm making more money, and that's great. But I feel like I'm neglecting the kids and I'm not sleeping well. And, I know I've been snapping at you more."

Lamar said, "Well..."

"Don't say anything. Just let me get this out," Sally said, "I need to work fewer hours. I don't know what the right amount is. I want to earn enough money to max out my IRA every year and help pay off the mortgage. I also want to put aside some money so we can travel. You know, take a vacation once in a while."

"That would be nice."

"I'm also thinking that we might be able to invest in something that would pay us now," Sally said. "Not wait until retirement. Maybe we could build up an account that would take the place of some of our income. Then we wouldn't have to depend on our jobs as much."

After a few seconds, Lamar said, "Sally, that all sounds great. But is it possible? I mean, it just doesn't seem realistic."

"I know," Sally said, "or rather, I don't know. But I'm going to do some research to find out. In the meantime, I'll keep up my IRA contributions and we'll apply all of the money that we were using to pay off credit cards to pay off the mortgage."

"Whew... I'm glad," Lamar said.

Scene 27, Saturday, 2/11, Year 4

Lamar closed the door of the gym locker. Then he slipped his left arm into the sleeve of his t-shirt. "I've been looking forward to playing racquetball all week," he said. "I need to work off some stress,"

"What's eating at you? I thought things were going pretty well. Did you and Sally have a fight?" Dick asked.

Dick sat down on the locker room bench. He reached over to tie his sneakers. Lamar sat beside him and shoehorned his right foot into his own sneaker.

"No. Nothing like that," Lamar said. "We're getting along good. But, you know, she keeps coming up with all these ideas to change things."

Dick gathered up his gym bag and pushed it into his locker.

Lamar continued, "Now, Sally wants to try to get income from investments. She wants to supplement our income from work. That's in addition to saving for retirement and paying off the mortgage. I just don't see how it can work. I'm afraid she's going to sabotage our retirement plan and delay paying off the mortgage."

"Is she doing something about it, or is she just talking?"

"Right now, she's doing research. Trying to see if there's any way to make it all work," Lamar said.

"Maybe it's too soon for you to be worried. She's got a pretty good head on her shoulders," Dick said. "If she does find a way to make it work, you'll be better off. And, it's a pretty interesting idea. I'm not sure how efficient it would be though. You'd have to pay taxes on the income, of course. And, there are IRS penalties if you withdraw money from an IRA or 401k before you turn 59 and ½. It's difficult to use a retirement account for current income until you're older."

Lamar clicked the padlock in place on his locker and said, "I just want to pay off the mortgage."

Dick picked up his racquet. "You're doing that, aren't you?" he asked. "You haven't even slowed down a bit. You're paying more every month than Jane and I are. We used some of our money to increase our 401k contributions."

Lamar picked up his equipment and turned toward the locker room door. "That's true," he said. "It just makes me nervous when Sally thinks up new stuff."

Dick said, "Lamar, you get nervous when she wants to change her hairstyle."

"Guilty as charged."

"Why don't we get together over dinner next weekend. We haven't done that in a while. I'd like to talk about this idea with everybody," Dick said as they entered the hallway.

"Sure. Sally will love that. Let's ask the wives to work out the details."

"Great!" Dick said. "Now prepare to be beaten!"

"Not likely," Lamar said. "I'm crackling with energy. I can't lose!"

"We'll see."

Scene 28, Sunday, 2/19, Year 4

Sally carefully rested a fragile stemmed wine glass on the end table. "I do like this Riesling," she said.

"Me to," Jane said, "Riesling is my favorite wine." She sighed. "With all the kids safely playing in the basement, we can relax and enjoy a few moments of peace."

Lamar swirled the much darker liquid in his glass and sipped. "I'm glad you two love the Riesling so much," he said. "That leaves a lot more Malbec for me and Dick."

"Here, here!" Dick affirmed. Then he looked at Sally and asked, "What's this we hear about you wanting to live off your investments, Sally?"

Sally looked up. "That's not exactly right. Think of this," she said. "What if we could gradually increase our current income from investments. The supplemental income could replace some of our work. We wouldn't have to work as many hours for the same income. Eventually, maybe it could replace work altogether." She leaned forward and plucked a cube of extra sharp cheddar from the silver tray on the coffee table.

Jane said, "That's called retirement, Sally."

"Jane's right," Dick said. "Pulling income from your retirement accounts will just slow down the process. It'll take longer for you to get enough money to retire on." Then he reached for a cube of cheese.

Lamar leaned back and sipped his wine.

Sally said, "I'm not talking about pulling money out of the retirement accounts. This would be a separate taxable account."

Lamar spoke softly, "Yeah, but it would be money that could have been put in the retirement accounts instead of this "taxable" account". How can it not delay our retirement?"

Sally hesitated and looked at her husband. "I suppose that's true," she said. "But maybe it's okay anyway. It kinda depends on what retirement is, exactly."

Lamar shook his head. He placed his wine glass on the end table and looked at his wife. "What does that mean? Retirement is not having to go to work. It's traveling when you want to. Puttering in the garden. Playing with the grandkids. That's what retirement is."

Dick peered over his wine glass and said, "That's not what my retirement will be. I want to do something productive, but on my own terms. Something creative and useful. But something that I'll really enjoy."

Jane looked at Dick and said, "Traveling and playing with the grandkids sounds pretty good to me." Then she looked at her empty glass and stood up. "I'm going to get more of that wonderful Riesling. I'll be right back."

Sally looked thoughtful. "That kind of retirement sounds good to me too," she said. "I want that and I want to keep doing useful work – just not as much of it. I guess I want to have my cake and eat it too. And I want some of it now. I don't want to wait thirty years."

"This working from home gig has spoiled you hasn't it?" Jane called from the kitchen.

Sally responded, "Yes. I like it that way. And, I want more of it."

Dick said, "It sounds like you want sort of an early semi-retirement."

Sally said, "Yes. That's a good way to put it."

"Maybe you could figure out how much extra income you'll need to fund a semi-retirement," Dick said. "Then you can decide if it's achievable. You might also throw in some calculations on how it would affect your retirement timetable."

Jane returned with her refilled glass, a bottle of Riesling and another of Malbec. She poured some Malbec for Dick. "Does anyone else want more wine?" she asked.

Sally offered her glass and said, "Yes, Riesling please."

Jane filled Sally's glass. Then she set the bottles on the coffee table. Turning to Dick she said, "What's our retirement timetable? How much money do we need to retire?"

Dick responded, "Good question. Before we can answer it, I think we need to figure out what we want our retirement to look like."

Lamar sipped his wine, then said, "It looks like we've got a lot of work to do on all of this."

"I guess you have to know what the target is before you can hit it," Sally said. "The roast will be done in a few more minutes. Let's set the table."

They all stood up and headed for the dining room.

Scene 29, Tuesday, 2/21, Year 4

Jane sat at the kitchen table tapping a pencil on a legal pad. Spot, lying on the kitchen floor in his favorite corner, pricked up his ears with each tap of the pencil.

Finally, Jane looked up. "I don't know how to start," she said. "Retirement is so far away. How are we supposed to know how much we'll need that far in the future? Everything changes. Some things get more expensive. Some things get cheaper. We change too. I don't know what I'm going to want for dinner tomorrow. How'm I supposed to know what I'll want to do in thirty years?"

As the screen on his laptop timed out and went dark, Dick looked across the table at his wife. He said, "You're right. I guess that's too much to expect. There are a lot of things I just don't care about anymore. Things I used to love to do. And some things I'm interested in today weren't even things ten years ago."

"Me too. I don't see the changes slowing down in the next thirty years either," Jane said. "So, how can we do this? It's just a shot in the dark."

Dick sat back in his chair and was silent for a moment. "Well," he said, "we know a few things. Maybe we can guess at a few more. Maybe that'll be enough."

"Huh. What exactly do we know?"

Dick said, "We know how much we spend right now. And we know how old our kids will be in thirty years. We also know, or we can find out, the average rate of inflation in the past."

"Okay, we certainly hope the kids are out on their own by then," Jane said. "That'll make our expenses less, for sure."

"We know we'll want to travel some and we can figure out how much that would cost today. That will increase our expenses," Dick said.

"When people get older," Jane said. "they need more health care. But no one knows what will happen to that. It could go up like a rocket or it could fall like a rock."

Dick said, "So, we'll just assume it stays the same as now. We shouldn't have to pay for the kid's health care then. Counting what we pay for the kids now gives us a little cushion. We can keep the same budget plus average inflation."

"How do we know what everything will cost then? It's bound to be different," Jane said.

"We can't know. But we can make a reasonable guess. We can add up the costs of the things we use now. Then factor in the historic average inflation."

Jane wrote the word 'inflation' on her legal pad and underlined it. "That's easy to say. But first, how do you factor in inflation anyway? And second, who says past inflation will be the same as future inflation? I just don't see the point to any of this."

"The first thing is easy," Dick said. "There's a formula called Future Value. It's used to figure out how much an amount you have now, will be worth at some point in the future. It assumes that the starting amount grows at a known constant rate. I don't know the formula, but it's built into Microsoft Excel. It's the FV function."

He woke up his computer and punched some keys. Then he turned it around so Jane could see the screen.

"Here's the FV function," he said. "It's pretty easy to use."

"I don't know much about inflation," Jane said, "but I know it changes every year. It's not constant."

"That's true," Dick said, "but the historic average is the average of all the high and low periods of inflation in the past. It's the number that gets you pretty close to the value today if you start with a value from twenty or thirty years ago. That sort of addresses your second point. Inflation will go up and down, but the future average will end up closer to the historic average than to the highs or the lows."

"But if it's higher in the future won't that hurt us?"

Dick replied, "Maybe we can use some fudge factors. We could assume a higher-than-average inflation rate. We could also set a target number higher than the future value calculation gives us. There will still be uncertainty, but it puts the odds in our favor. Plus, we can tweak the plan as things change."

Spot arose from his corner and shook himself thoroughly.

"What do you mean by a 'target number'?" Jane asked.

"Our target number is the amount of money we think we'll need to give us the income we want during our retirement."

"That doesn't make sense," she said. "We don't even know how much money we would need to give us our current income, let alone what we'll need in thirty years."

Spot laid his head on Jane's knee and she automatically started stroking his head.

Dick said, "Well, we kind of do. We at least know that government bonds are paying about 2% interest. And we know stock dividends are paying about 2.5% on average. So, it seems to me that the worst case is we would need enough money to generate our current monthly income at a 2.5% interest rate. That's for today. Then, we could put that number through the future value formula to get our target number in thirty years."

Jane didn't answer. She just shook her head. "That's a lot to think about. I need to digest it all."

"Sure," Dick said. Let me see if I can model what we've talked about on a spreadsheet. Then, after you've had time to think about it, we can look at the model."

"Okay," Jane said. "I'm going to make some coffee."

"Sounds good."

Scene 30, Saturday, 2/25, Year 4

Calvin pushed away his breakfast dishes. "I'm done, Mom!" he said. "Can I go now? Please? I wanna watch my Saturday morning shows!"

"Alright, Calvin. You may leave the table," Sally said.

Calvin scooted his chair away from the kitchen table and rushed out of the room. Marie said, "Me too!' and started to follow.

Lamar put his arm up to block her path. "Not so fast young lady," he said. "You haven't finished your breakfast."

"But Calvin got to go," Marie complained.

"Calvin finished his breakfast," Lamar said.

"But I'm not hungry anymore!"

Lamar looked at Sally. Sally stood up and picked up Marie's nearly empty plate. She said, "Finish your juice, then you can leave the table."

Marie quickly slurped her remaining orange juice. "Thanks, Mom!' she yelled as she ran after her brother.

Lamar pushed back from the table and carried his breakfast dishes to the sink. Sally started rinsing the dishes and stacking them in the dishwasher.

Lamar cleared the rest of the table and wiped it with a damp cloth.

Sally said, "Why don't you bring the laptop in here while I finish up the dishes? Then we can think about how I can work fewer hours"

"Okay," Lamar said without enthusiasm.

A few minutes later, Lamar carried a laptop computer, a mouse, and a power cord into the room. He started organizing the equipment on the kitchen table and plugging in cables.

"That coffee smells good," he said.

Sally replied, "I started a fresh pot. It'll be ready in a few minutes."

Lamar sat in front of the computer and adjusted his chair. "Okay. I'm ready," he said. "I'll capture the numbers in a spreadsheet to make it easy to do the math."

"Right. So, here's the background," Sally said. "It varies, but I work about 48 hours per week.

Lamar's fingers danced over the keyboard producing clicking sounds.

"The average profit from my business is about $600 per week. But I plan to take two weeks off every year. So, I'll work 50 weeks per year, not 52."

Lamar stopped typing. He looked up and said, "That's $30,000 of profit per year."

Sally said, "I'd like to work half that much, 24 hours per week. That means I need to replace $15,000 of income."

Lamar said, "The average dividend yield from common stock is about 2.5%. $15,000 divided by 2.5% is $600,000."

"Wow! That's a lot," Sally said.

"That's impossible Sally. If you need $600,000 to replace $15,000 of income, how much do we need to retire? Ten million?"

"Maybe there are better ways to generate income from investments."

"I sure hope so," Lamar said, "or we'll never be able to retire. And you sure won't replace $15,000 of income anytime soon."

"Let's do some research. There must be a better answer."

"Well, we have the time. We have the computer. We have Google. And, now, we have coffee. Can I get you some, Sally?" Lamar got up and walked to the coffee pot."

"Yes, please. This could take a while."

Scene 31, Saturday, 2/25, Year 4

Sally had her head down reading intently. She was focused on one of the two laptop computers open on the kitchen table. Her husband was staring just as intently at the other one.

The sound of her daughter's footsteps on the kitchen tile pulled her attention back into 'mother mode'. She looked up from her computer screen just in time to see Marie stop in front of the refrigerator.

"Can I have a popsicle, Mom?" her daughter asked.

Sally looked her in the eyes and waited expectantly.

"Eh, please, Mom? Can I have a popsicle?"

Sally scooted back from the table and walked to the refrigerator.

"You can have one, Honey. But you have to eat it in here. I don't want it dripping all over the living room carpet," Sally said.

"I promise I won't drip."

"Don't make promises you can't keep, Marie," Sally said as she opened the freezer door.

She found the popsicles and as she removed one, she said, "What have you learned about annuities Lamar?"

"Marie, come over here and sit by me while you eat your popsicle, Honey."

Marie ran around the table to the empty chair next to her father.

"All the charts I found start at age 40," Lamar said. "It looks like you can't buy an immediate annuity until you're at least 40 years old. Anyway, we need some time to save the money, so I got estimates for every five years starting at age 41. The percentage payouts don't seem to change when you increase the amount invested.

"I won't be 41 until May of next year," Sally said. "I don't want to wait that long. Well, what will it do for us when I'm 41?"

"A $100,000 investment returns $311 per month or $3,732 per year. Since that's like a 3.732% interest rate, we'd need $402,000 to replace $15,000 per year of income. Of course, to cover inflation, we'd need more than that. Here's the whole chart."

Sally examined the spreadsheet for a few moments. Then she said, "It looks like the yields increase steadily as you get older. When I'm 51 the $100,000 would yield $4,212. And when I'm 66 it would be $5,136."

Lamar watched a drip from his daughter's popsicle run down her hand. He reached across the table for a paper napkin and handed it to her. "Here, Honey. Try not to get too sticky."

Then he turned his attention back to his wife. "Yeah," he said. Even when you're 66 it would take about $300,000 to produce $15,000 of income."

"That's disappointing," she said. "When the interest rate gets over 5%, in our 60's, it might be worth thinking about, but it's not going to help my early semi-retirement plan. We have to keep looking."

"Dad, what's a interest rate?" Marie asked.

Lamar chuckled. He looked at Sally questioningly.

Sally said, "Don't look at me. She asked you," and laughed.

Lamar said, "Well...."

Scene 32, Saturday, 2/25, Year 4

The deep resinous voice of an audiobook narrator was the only sound coming from the living room.

Jane silently looked in that direction for a few seconds.

Dick looked at his wife and said, "The boys seem to be enthralled by 'Treasure Island', don't they?"

"Yes. Finding that free audiobook website was a real coup," Jane said. "What was the name of it again?"

"I don't remember the URL, but you can find it by searching for 'The LibriVox Free Audiobook Collection'. Of course, it only has books in the public domain, so they're all quite old."

"That's okay. It's a great way to expose the twins to classic literature."

"Speaking of classics," Dick said, "and returning to our topic, I discovered that Financial Planners have this thing they call a safe withdrawal rate."

"That sounds good. I like safe. What is it?"

Dick said, "It's a percentage they figure is safe to withdraw from your retirement savings every year without running out of money before you die."

"Is that the 'spend it all so your kids don't get any' plan? That doesn't sound very safe."

"No. The classic plan is pretty simple but the justification is complicated," Dick said. "Some guy did a lot of statistical testing of thousands of different scenarios using historic market data with a lot of different start and endpoints. They call it a Monte Carlo analysis. The idea was to find a plan that would survive the worst cases."

"Did he find one then?"

"Kind of," Dick replied, "but it has some holes. The safe withdrawal rate plan he came up with is supposed to give you a 95% probability of still having money left over after a thirty-year retirement."

"What about the other 5% of the time?"

"That's one problem. Another problem is that people are living longer. A lot of people will live more than thirty years after they retire. There's a third problem too. If you happen to retire during a time, like now, when interest rates are very low and the stock market is high – well, that puts you at the bad end of the statistics. So, the probability of your money lasting thirty years goes down. I don't know by how much though."

Jane said, "It doesn't sound all that safe then."

"No. But it gives us a place to start. Sort of a baseline plan. One we know we have to beat."

"Well, what is this not so safe - safe withdrawal rate plan?" Jane asked.

"In the original, classic, version you withdraw 4% of the value of your savings in the first year of retirement," Dick said. "That's a specific amount of money. It depends on how much savings you have, but at that moment in time, it's a fixed amount. Let's call it $50,000."

"Since we're dreaming, let's call it $100,000."

"Okay," Dick said. "We'll pretend 4% of our retirement savings is $100,000. That's how much you withdraw the first year. If at the end of the first-year, inflation was 3%, then the second year you'd withdraw $103,000 or 3% more than the first year. If inflation during the second year was 4%, you withdraw 4% more for the third year or about $107,000. Say inflation goes down to 1% for the third year. Then, you only take out another 1% for the fourth year. That would bring your withdrawal up to about $108,000. It continues like that for the rest of your retirement."

Jane was quiet for a moment. Then she said. "If you withdraw 4% a year, your money would last twenty-five years. But this plan starts at 4% and goes up every year. I would think the money would run out in ten to fifteen years."

"That would be true if you never earned interest or dividends and the value of your investments never increased," Dick said. "The reason the plan works is that your portfolio continues to earn more money. It becomes a race to see if you earn more than you withdraw. In a lot of the tested scenarios the value of the portfolio is higher after thirty years than it was at the start."

"What if your expenses go up more than inflation?"

"That's yet a fourth problem. That could make the withdrawals lose the race. Or maybe it's better to say it could make us lose the race," Dick said. "But there are several ways we could make the plan safer. One way would be to withdraw less than 4% in the first year and keep everything else the same. Another way is to reduce your spending when the market goes down. For example, you could take a pass on the inflation adjustment any year the market goes down."

"That makes more sense. I wouldn't want to watch our savings go to zero without doing something about it," Jane said.

"Yeah, I agree. Eventually, we'll have to figure out how we'll do this. But it's not an immediate crisis."

"I'm getting bored with this," Jane said. "Can we continue the retirement planning conversation later?"

"Sure. Can I have a slice of that apple pie now? How are the plans for the surprise party coming?"

Jane said, "We'll both have pie. If you cut it for us. I'll make coffee."

Jane started priming the coffee pot while Dick removed the pie from the refrigerator.

"This morning Jacob said two of his classmates told him they're coming to his birthday party next Saturday."

"Ouch!" Dick said. "There goes the surprise. I guess it was inevitable. It's hard to keep a secret when so many people are involved."

"Yeah. But it should be a great party anyway. Between them, Jacob and John have a lot of friends."

Scene 33, Saturday, 2/25, Year 4

Sally looked up from her computer and glanced at the kitchen sink. It was full of dishes from lunch. She sighed and tapped her finger on the table.

"What's wrong?" Lamar asked.

"Nothing. I'm just a little distracted by the lunch dishes. I hate to leave them in the sink."

"I'll tell you what. I'll do the dishes while you keep working." Lamar pushed away from his computer and headed for the sink.

Sally sighed again. "Thank you," she said. "That helps."

Lamar filled the sink with hot soapy water. Then he asked, "Have you found anything interesting yet?"

"Maybe," she replied. "It turns out the average dividend rate people talk about is the average dividends paid by the companies in the S&P500 index."

"That's like the 500 biggest companies in the world, right?"

Sally hesitated before answering, "Not quite. It's 500 of the biggest companies listed on US stock exchanges. There's some kind of committee that decides what companies are part of the list. People don't always agree with the committee. But it doesn't matter. The index resembles the whole American stock market. The thing is though, about half of the companies in the index don't even pay dividends. So, the average dividend rate is skewed downward."

Lamar did some quick mental arithmetic. Then he said, "If you only buy stocks that pay dividends you could get a 5% yield! You'd still need $300,000, but that's a lot better than $600,000."

Sally said, "Yeah. Also, I understand there are some companies that get special tax breaks if they pay out most of their earnings in dividends. Maybe they pay even more than 5%. I'm going to check that out next."

Their son, Calvin, stood at the kitchen door and looked at his parents. "How long are you guys gonna keep doing this boring stuff?" he asked. "I wanna go somewhere and do something."

"How would you like to go to the YMCA with me?" Lamar asked. "I'm meeting Dick there for racquetball in an hour. The Y has an open basketball court all afternoon. You could shoot some hoops while I'm playing racquetball."

"Great! Can we go now?" Calvin asked.

"You can change your clothes while I do the dishes. We'll leave in about twenty minutes."

"That's good Lamar," Sally said. "I'll take Marie with me. I need to go shopping and I need a break from this stuff too."

Scene 34, Sunday, 2/26, Year 4

Dick scanned the traffic on Rosemont Avenue and said, "It's been a pleasant day so far, don't you think, Jane?"

"Yes," Jane replied, "the worship service was uplifting and the sermon was challenging. Just the way they should be."

"Lunch was fun too!" offered Jacob.

"It was, wasn't it?" Dick said as he turned on the radio.

They drove quietly for a few minutes, listening to a radio program.

After a while, Jane reached for the dashboard and turned the radio off. She said, "That Mel On Money guy just said, 'diversification is the only free lunch'. He didn't explain what it means though. Have you heard that one Dick?"

Dick changed his grip on the steering wheel and glanced at his wife. "It's what I've been researching lately," he said. "There's this thing called 'Modern Portfolio Theory' or MPT. It's been successfully used and misused since the 1950s..."

"Let's stick with 'diversification'. What does it mean?" Jane interrupted.

Dick paused. "Right. Okay." He thought for a few seconds. Then he said, "Diversification means having your money in different kinds of things. Different enough that when the value of one of them falls or crashes the rest are unaffected. Or they might even go up. The classic case is stocks and bonds, especially U.S. Treasury Bonds. When the stock market crashes, the value of U.S. Treasury Bonds usually goes up. Mostly because people buy them because they're safe. But also, the Federal Reserve generally cuts interest rates when the market crashes. That makes the price of bonds go up too."

"That makes sense," Jane said, "But why is it a 'free lunch'?"

Dick delayed his response as he made a left turn. Then he said, "That brings me back to Modern Portfolio Theory (MPT). Are you ready to talk about that?"

"Huh. Okay," Jane said reluctantly. "Go ahead,"

"I won!" shouted a voice from the backseat.

"You were just lucky," another voice sounded. "I'll win next time."

"We'll see," taunted the first voice.

"Boys," Dick said, "Keep it down, please. Your Mother and I are having a conversation."

"Yes sir," they said in unison.

Dick cleared his throat. "Well," he said, "the basic idea is that if you have a portfolio – a group of different investments – made up of things that are not correlated ..."

"Wait a minute." She shook her head, "What's correlated mean?"

"Sorry," Dick said. "Correlated means they go up or down together. Correlation is a measurement of how well they track each other - or go up and down together. So, if things are not correlated, then they don't go up and down together. If they're negatively correlated, then when one goes up the other goes down – like the stocks and bonds I was talking about a while ago. Does that help?"

Jane stared out the windshield for a few seconds. Then she said, "Okay. You want a group of investments that go up and down independently from each other. Is that right?"

"Perfect," Dick said. "If you have a portfolio like that and you rebalance it once in a while..."

"Stop! You did it again. What does rebalance mean?"

"Yeah. Well," Dick said, "you have this portfolio of different investments. When you set it up, you decide how much of each one you want in the portfolio. It's easiest to use percentages. To keep it simple, let's say you have four different investments. You want each one to be 25% of the portfolio. That's the way you set it up when you buy the securities."

"Dick," Jane said, "this is painful, like learning a foreign language. Define securities, please."

"Right," Dick said. "A security is the thing you actually buy on the stock exchange. It's a way to show you have ownership of a bit of whatever it represents - like a stock represents ownership of a bit of a company. But the stock isn't the actual company. Pretty much everything available to buy through a stockbroker is a security. Anyway, in the example, we initially buy four securities and each one represents a different kind of investment. Each different kind is called an 'asset class'. We put 25% of the money into stocks, 25% into U.S. Treasury Bonds, 25% into gold, and keep 25% in cash. Four different asset classes. What do you think will happen over the next year?"

"How should I know? Things change. They go up and down."

"That's exactly right," Dick said. "Things change and we can't predict how they'll change. But it doesn't matter. Something went up and something went down. To keep things clear, let's assume the stocks went up and the gold went down. The bonds and cash stayed the same – near enough. In this case, you would sell some of the stocks and buy more gold. Enough so that each of the four asset classes is brought back to 25% of the new total value. That's what it means to rebalance. To put the portfolio back to its original percentages."

"It doesn't seem right to sell the stocks when they're going up."

"I know it feels wrong," Dick said. "But MPT says it's the right thing to do. If you rebalance consistently over a long time, the whole portfolio will do better than any of its separate parts. And when it goes down, it won't go down as much."

"It sounds like you think this rebalancing a diversified portfolio is a good thing. Do you think it's the way we should manage our retirement accounts?' Jane asked.

"Yes. I do," Dick replied. "I need to do more research on the details. But this seems like the safest and surest bet."

"Does the diversified portfolio thing work with the safe withdrawal rate?"

"Yup. They're completely separate ideas," Dick said. "The diversified portfolio, or rather rebalancing a diversified portfolio, is a way to manage your long-term investments. The safe withdrawal rate is a way to manage living off your investment money. Regardless of how you manage the investments. They work together perfectly to keep your money safe and growing."

Dick pulled the car into their driveway and stopped. Immediately, the twins rushed out with doors slamming.

Dick said, "I think they're in a hurry to get out of their church clothes."

Jane looked at her husband. "I'm looking forward to it too," she said.

Scene 35, Sunday, 2/26, Year 4

Lamar walked into the kitchen with Marie giggling on his back. He stopped in front of the refrigerator and waited as Marie opened the top freezer door.

Sally looked up from her computer screen. "She wore you down, I see."

"What can I say. It's popsicle time."

"I got grape!" Marie said proudly. "Here Daddy. You can have orange."

"Thank you, Honey," Lamar said. "Will you hold onto my orange until I get us settled in at the table?"

"Okay," Marie agreed.

"Do you want a popsicle, Sally?" Lamar asked.

"Yes, please. Can you find a raspberry for me, Marie?

"Sure, Mom," Marie happily rummaged through the freezer and pulled out a red popsicle. "I found one!"

Lamar pulled a chair out for Marie and maneuvered her around his shoulder onto it. Then he pulled one out for himself. He said, "Have you figured out the differences between those special kinds of companies, Sally?"

"Here, Daddy. Here's your orange."

"Thanks, Honey." Lamar sat down and peeled the paper from his popsicle.

"Here's your raspberry, Mom."

"Thank you, Marie," Sally said as she received the icy treat.

"I haven't figured it all out yet. But the main differences seem to be their names and what they invest in. The Real Estate Investment Trust, known as a REIT, is a really broad category. They invest in anything related to real estate. Some REITs own shopping malls, apartments, single-family homes, cell phone towers, or just mortgages instead of the actual property. Master Limited Partnerships, MLPs for short, usually own pipelines or oil and natural gas wells. And Business Development Companies, or BDCs, loan money to small and medium-sized businesses – kind of like a bank would."

"Do they all pay high dividends?" Lamar asked. Then he bit off a chunk of his popsicle.

Sally broke her popsicle in half. "Mostly," she said. "They're all required by law to payout 80% of their earnings as dividends. Sometimes they make extra payments to shareholders called a 'return of capital'. I don't understand it very well, but it seems to make income taxes a bit more complicated. The thing is, most of these companies pay much higher dividends than normal companies. As high as 7 to 10% compared to the 1 to 5% for most regular dividend-paying companies."

Lamar paused his popsicle in mid-air. "Wow! That's a big improvement. At a 10% rate, you'd only need $150,000 to get $15,000 of income. I don't think you're gonna do much better than that."

"Yeah. I've seen a few other things that might be as good. But none better."

"What other things?" Lamar asked.

"I saw a couple of things that look like funds of some kind that have dividend yields comparable to the REITs, MLPs, and BDCs. I don't know much about them yet," Sally said. "But I'll research them too."

"That's good," Lamar said. "Better to have a lot of good options.

"Whoa!" Sally said as she handed Marie a paper napkin. "Wipe your hand, Marie, before the juice drips all over."

Scene 36, Monday, 2/27, Year 4

"It's after 9. How much longer are you gonna be?" Jane asked.

"I guess I'm about done for the evening. I've been learning a lot," Dick said. "I'm wondering if we should move our Roth IRA money out of mutual funds and into ETFs. Using that diversified portfolio rebalancing that we talked about yesterday."

"I'm going to brew some of that Twinning's Decaffeinated English Breakfast Tea. Would you like a cup?"

Dick looked up from the computer screen and said, "Absolutely! It's the best."

Jane put the kettle on to boil. Then she said, "I understand what a mutual fund is. All of our 401k money is invested in mutual funds. But what's an ETF? Aren't they the same thing?"

Dick leaned back in his chair. "What I found out, is an ETF or Exchange Traded Fund, is like a mutual fund but different. It's like a mutual fund because it groups together a selection of different investments - company stocks for example. And, like a mutual fund, ETFs can have different strategies. Their strategies determine what kinds of securities the fund holds."

"So, what makes them different?"

"For some reason," Dick said, "the fees charged by ETFs are almost always lower than on similar mutual funds, even when they are both from the same company. Because of the lower fees, ETFs tend to do better over the long-term."

"That sounds good,"

"Another big difference is the timing of trades. You know that when you buy or sell a mutual fund the trade happens after the market closes. You don't find out what price you got until the next day."

"Yeah. That's always troubled me."

"Well, an Exchange Traded Fund, like the name implies, trades on the stock exchange just like a common stock. That means you can use limit orders to control your price. It also means the trade can happen immediately. There are other differences that I don't understand. Mostly they have to do with which SEC rules apply and how they're allowed to charge fees."

The teapot whistled and Jane moved it to an open burner. She put tea bags in two cups and poured.

"Anyway," Dick continued, "for us, trading in real-time on the exchange and especially controlling the price, are the important differences."

Jane put one cup in front of Dick along with a bowl of Stevia. She set her cup on the table and retrieved a bottle of Almond Milk from the refrigerator. As she sat down across from Dick, she said, "Uh... What's a limit order?"

Dick stirred a spoonful of Stevia into his tea. "Yeah. Okay, more jargon." He paused with a thoughtful look on his face. "It's pretty simple. It's like the difference between going to the store or going to the flea market. A 'market order' is like the flea market. There, you expect to bargain. You don't know what price you'll pay at first because the seller has to agree with you on the price."

"Is it kind of like an auction?"

"It is an auction. You offer your stock for sale and everyone interested in buying it offers a price. The best price buys the stock. In the old days, there were literally people on the floor of the exchange offering and bidding in person by voice. Now, of course, it's all done by computer somehow."

"All right. I think I understand a market order," Jane said. "What about the limit thing?"

A limit order is like going to the store where the price is fixed and you either take it or leave it," Dick said. "If you're buying, you either pay the price on the label or you wait to buy it at your price somewhere else. A limit order says you're only willing to buy or sell a stock at your price or better. If you're buying, better means lower than the limit price.

If you're selling, better means higher than your limit price. Does that help?"

Jane removed her teabag from her cup and sipped. "I think so," she said. "You're saying if I sell a stock for $10 using a limit order, then I will get at least $10 when it sells."

"Exactly. The downside is that you don't know when it will sell. Just like you don't know when a shopper will want to buy the pound of hamburger on the store shelf."

"So, it's like when the seller puts a reserve price on at an auction. If the bid doesn't beat the reserve price the seller keeps the item."

"That's right. Although in this case a buyer gets to use the reserve idea too."

"I get it now. It really is simple if you think of it like that," Jane said. "You can buy and sell ETFs using limit orders? That's how you control the price?"

"You got it," Dick said. "And that all ties in with diversified portfolio rebalancing. You can use limit orders to control the price when you rebalance. That gives you more control of the process. You can bring your percentage allocations back in line more precisely."

Dick paused and looked at his wife. "You know," he said, "answering your questions has made me get very clear about ETFs. Now I'm convinced we should move out of mutual funds and into ETFs as much as possible."

Dick sipped his tea. "This is good. When you discovered Twinning's English Breakfast Tea it was a real coup!"

Jane smiled. "It is good, isn't it?" she said. "Why don't you put that away now. I want you to watch my program with me."

"Sure. It'll just take a minute to shut down my laptop."

Scene 37, Tuesday, 2/28, Year 4

"I'm glad the kids could agree on a movie to watch," Lamar said. "That should give us an hour or so to talk about this investing stuff."

Sally said, "Cartoon movies usually do the trick. And I do need to tell you what I learned about alternatives."

"I think I understand the ETFs for REITs, MLPs, and BDCs now, Sally," Lamar said. "But what's an 'alternative'. I mean, I know it's something different – an alternative – but when you say it, you make it sound like it's not just another choice, but some special investment class."

Sally sipped her ice water. "I don't understand it all that well," she said. "It kind of means both things. They seem to use the word as a catch-all. Any investment that doesn't fit neatly into a classic asset class they'll call an alternative." At the sound of laughter, she turned her head toward the living room doorway.

Lamar wrapped his hand around the plastic bottle of Diet Coke resting on the table. When the laughter from the living room died down, he tilted his head slightly to the right. "Okay," he said. "There are classic asset classes like stocks, bonds, precious metals, commodities, real estate, and currencies." He paused and took a pull from the Diet Coke. "Anything else would be an 'Alternative' investment or asset class?"

"Yeah. That's about right. The investing community lumps everything else into one asset class they generally call 'alternatives', even though there are a lot of very different strategies available within the group." She watched as her husband tried to make sense of it all.

"Look," she said, "the possible strategies that qualify as an 'alternative' is endless. We're not going to understand them all. We don't have to. We only have to understand the ones we decide to use. And, so far at least, there's only one that seems useful. Let's just focus on it."

"There's so much stuff to know," Lamar said. "How can anyone keep up with it all?"

"They can't, Lamar. That's why even the pros who spend 80 hours a week immersed in it have to specialize. They learn their piece of the business deeply and stick to it."

"So, I guess we have to learn our little piece and stick to it too. Is that the answer, Sally?"

Marie's giggles interrupted the conversation momentarily.

Sally looked toward the living room and smiled. She turned back to Lamar and said, "I believe it is." After sipping some ice water, she continued, "There's one kind of alternative investment that looks promising to me. I found several ETFs that pay dividends between 9 and 10%. They make their money investing in common stock and offering options contracts on them. They call it a 'Buy-Write' strategy."

"Do you even know what that means, Sally? I sure don't."

"Not completely. I don't understand how they make money using option contracts. But I know their prices and their dividends have been pretty stable over several years. They seem to be good at what they're doing."

"That's something anyway," Lamar said.

"I'm thinking about a portfolio of four to six ETFs. Only one would be an Alternative. The rest would be REITs, MLPs, BDCs, and maybe one or two more regular ETFs with higher-than-average dividend yields. The way I figure it, we can easily average more than a 7% yield."

Lamar quickly pecked at the calculator app on his phone. "$15,000 divided by 7% is $214,000," he said. "No matter how you cut it it's still a big number Sally."

"Yes. It is. And I don't think we can plan on getting more than 7% dividends. $214,000 is still too much. What can I do? I don't want to give up on early semi-retirement."

"Take a couple of days to think about it Sally, Lamar said. "You'll come up with something. You always do."

"Right. I'll find a way."

At that moment the cuckoo clock in the living room indicated eight o'clock.

Sally smiled and said, "It's Marie's bedtime. And, it's your turn to read her a story. Go do your daddy duty."

"Okay. I'm on it."

Scene 38, Saturday, 3/4, Year 4

"Hey, Lamar," Sally called from the kitchen.

Lamar stopped in mid-sentence. "Just a minute Marie, let me see what your mother wants, he said. "What do you need, my Love? I'm reading to Marie."

"I know. When you finish the chapter can you come in here for a bit? We need to talk."

"Oooo-kay. I'll be there in a couple of minutes," he said. "Marie, Honey, when we finish this chapter, we have to go see what Mommy needs. Would you like to get something to drink then?"

"Okay yes," Marie said. "I want a Coke,"

"It's too early for Coke. How about a glass of apple juice?"

"Okay. Read Daddy."

Sally waited.

She tapped her fingers on the table.

She got up and poured a cup of coffee.

She placed the coffee cup on the table beside her computer, but she didn't sit. Instead, she paced the room.

Finally, she heard her husband say, "And that's the end of the chapter."

Marie jumped off her father's lap and ran into the kitchen. "I'm gonna have apple juice, Mommy."

"Yes, you are. Sit at the table and I'll pour."

Sally took a glass from the cabinet as Lamar walked into the room. He poured himself a cup of coffee, and sat down next to Marie.

Sally set a glass of apple juice in front of her daughter. Then she turned to her husband.

"I'm trying to face reality, Lamar. I know this is stressful for you, but bear with me," Sally walked to the sink and looked out the window. Then she turned toward Lamar again.

"I'm okay Sally. I know you'll do the right thing. Please, come and sit down."

"Right. No pressure there."

She sat in front of her computer and picked up her neglected coffee. Took a sip and set it down. She said, "I've been working 48 hours a week and earning $30,000 a year. $30,000 divided by 48 is $625 in annual earnings per weekly hour worked." She paused.

"That's a strange way to look at it, Sally. Where are you going with this?"

"I'm trying to find a workable compromise between coming up with $214,000 and continuing to work 48 hours a week. I need to talk this through. Just hear me."

"Sure," Lamar said. He sipped his coffee and leaned back in his chair.

Marie put down her half-finished glass and ran out of the kitchen.

Sally looked at her computer screen. "$30,000 divided by 48 hours per week is $625 in annual earnings per weekly hour worked."

"I understand the arithmetic, but what does it mean."

"It means that every $625 of income we can generate from investments will replace one hour of work per week for a year," Sally said. "$625 in annual investment income would allow me to work 47 hours per week instead of 48."

"Oh. I get it," Lamar said,

$625 times 8 is $5,000 in annual earnings per 8 hours worked each week. That's one standard workday."

"So, that means if we can generate $5,000 in annual investment income you would only have to work 40 hours per week instead of 48, right?"

"Yeah, Sally said. "$5,000 divided by 7% is $71,500. If we had $71,500 invested in a portfolio of ETF's, like we talked about the other day, it would generate at least $5,000 in dividends each year."

Lamar took a sip of coffee and looked at the ceiling. After a few seconds, he said, "I think we could do that. As long as you agree to stop when we hit the 71,500 mark, I'd be okay with diverting some of our retirement savings and extra mortgage payments to make it happen faster."

"Thank you, Lamar," Sally said. "Once we get to the target number, then, if I can add to it from my business income every month it could keep growing. Maybe, eventually, it would produce enough to cut back another whole eight-hour day."

Lamar said, "That's a good plan. You get a little relief quickly and the hope of more in the future."

"It would eventually just become part of our retirement income," Sally said. "There'd be no reason to ever stop it."

"Perfect. Let's do it!"

Scene 39, Saturday, 3/4, Year 4

"What remains to be done to get ready for the birthday party, my Love?" Dick asked.

"We just have to get everything out and set the dining room table," Jane replied." The cake is decorated. Even the candles are on it. The thing that will take the most time is tying the helium balloons to the backs of the chairs."

"I'm glad we got the helium balloons this year. Blowing up all those balloons was a real chore."

Jane chuckled. "Yes. And it took a long time. I think we can get everything done today in about thirty minutes. But I'd like to get started an hour before the party, just to be sure."

"That makes sense. So, we have some time to think about retirement planning. Are you ready?" he asked.

"Yes, let's work on that for a while," Jane said.

"I'll set up my laptop." Dick left the room and returned a minute later with his laptop backpack.

As Dick set up his computer Jane said, "We've got a general idea of how we're going to manage our investments. And how we'll make withdrawals for retirement income." She paused and sipped her coffee. "But how much money do we need in order to retire?"

Dick inclined his head to the left and looked at his wife. "Hmmm," he said. "It's kind of the same question Lamar and Sally are struggling with, only bigger and farther in the future. I have a spreadsheet here I've been working on. It's coming up now."

"But Sally knows she wants to replace $15,000 of income right now. We don't know how much income we'll need in thirty years."

Dick said, "We might know enough to make a decent guess. Right now, our combined income is $68,000 a year. We're saving 20,000 for retirement. And we're paying 12,000 a year on our mortgage."

"We'll have the mortgage paid off way before thirty years, Jane said. "We won't have to make mortgage payments after we retire."

"Right. And we won't have to save for retirement either. We'll be retired."

Jane selected the calculator app on her phone and started tapping. "68,000 minus the 12,000 for mortgage payments and minus the 20,000 for retirement savings is only $36,000 a year," she said.

"We also talked about a few other changes we know about. The kids will be adults. Health care may cost more. And, we want to travel."

"But we don't know how those changes will affect us."

"No. We don't. But we know we'll spend less with the kids gone. And we know if we travel a lot, we'll spend more. So, they kind of cancel each other out."

"And health care is a complete unknown."

"So, let's assume it stays the same. Then we can just use an annual income of $36,000 as our baseline," Dick said. "According to the US Bureau of Labor Statistics[1] website, the historic inflation rate is 2.23% per year. Using the Future Value (FV) function in Microsoft Excel over thirty years makes our future income number 69,800."

Just then Jacob appeared in the kitchen doorway. He said, "We're going over to Ken's house and play board games."

"Okay, Dear, Jane said. "But don't go anywhere else, and be home by 4 o'clock. You don't want to miss your birthday party."

"We will, Mom. Bye," Jacob said as they ran out the front door.

Jane stood and brought the coffee pot to the table. She poured for Dick and herself.

Dick said, "Thanks, my Love."

Jane put the pot on the burner and returned to the table. "69,800 is the amount of income we'd need if inflation is average. What if it's higher than average?" she asked.

---

1.   https://www.bls.gov/cpi/

"I thought about that. I worked out a few scenarios in this spreadsheet," Dick said. "If inflation averages 3% for the next thirty years our income number would increase to 87,400. At 4% it would be 116,800."

"Wow! That's a big difference."

"Yeah, it is a big difference. I don't think inflation is likely to average 4% over thirty years though. Let's use 3.5% as a pretty safe worst case guess. Using 3.5% in the FV function predicts our income number will be 101,000," Dick said. "$100,000 per year is a nice round number and close enough. Can we use that as our target?"

"Okay," Jane said, nodding her head. "How does Social Security figure into this? Lots of people say it won't be there for us."

Dick sipped his coffee. Then he said, "Yeah. I hear that all the time. But you also hear how they're gonna have a universal basic income. Anyway, Social Security just works too well for it to go away. I read that the money going into the program is about 70% of the total cost. I think it's likely they'll figure out a way to fully fund it. But if they don't, a benefit cut of 30% seems like the worst case.

"Let's use the worst-case then. If that happened, we would only get 70% of what the annual statement says, right?"

"That's right," Dick said. "On our last statements, your projected monthly benefit was $1,200 and mine was $1,500. Together that's $2,700 per month or $32,400 per year. I don't think that includes the annual cost of living increases. It certainly doesn't include the salary increases we'll get over the years. But let's just use that number."

Jane tapped on her calculator app again. "32,400 times 70% is 22,700. 100,000 minus 22,700 is $77,300." She looked up at her husband. "That must be how much we'll need to get from our retirement savings," she said.

Dick typed on his keyboard, "Right. Using the 2.5% average dividend rate for the S&P500 index, that means we'd need 77,300 divided by 2.5% or $3,100,000."

"What? That can't be right!"

"Let's stop for now," Dick suggested. "I need to process some sticker shock."

"Good idea. Why don't we start getting ready for the birthday party early? Then we'll have time to relax before everyone comes over at 5 pm."

"That sounds like a good plan," Dick agreed, and he started to shut down his laptop.

Scene 40, Sunday, 3/5, Year 4

"It feels good to just sit back on the couch for a few minutes," Jane said.

"Yes, it does," Dick agreed. "With the birthday party yesterday and church this morning, it's been a busy 24 hours. Can I get you something to drink?"

"Hmmm, Yes. I'd like a glass of wine,"

"That does sound good. The Malbec? I think I'll have some of that." Malbec would be lovely,"

Dick headed purposefully to the kitchen just as the twins rounded the corner from the hallway at the end of the room.

Jacob said, "We're going to Ken's house, Mom."

"Not before you clean your room, you're not!"

"Aw, Mom!" said Jacob.

"We'll do it when we get back," John said.

"You'll do it now. And let's review. What does clean your room mean?"

"Put everything in its place," said Jacob.

"Vacuum the floor," said John.

"Dust the furniture," said Jacob.

"And bring all the dirty clothes to the laundry room," finished John.

"Right," said Jane. "Now hop to it." The boys ran to their room to get started. The sooner to join their friends at Ken's house.

In another minute, Dick returned carrying two wine glasses three-quarters full of the dark Argentine Malbec. He stretched his left arm toward his wife. "Here you are, my Love," he said.

"Thanks, Dick." Jane received the glass and immediately touched it to her lips. Dick rested his glass on the coffee table and cautiously sat down beside Jane.

"Now that things have calmed down. That 3.1-million-dollar figure keeps coming back. I can't get it out of my mind. How can we possibly save that much money before we retire?"

"Well, it might be possible," Dick said. "Compounding can do amazing things over long periods. That's why it's called the eighth wonder of the world. But we won't want to live on 'beans and rice and rice and beans' for the next thirty years."

"What can we do then?"

"First, I guess we should find out if it's a reasonable goal or not," Dick said. "We can run our current savings rate through the Excel FV function and see what we're likely to end up with if we keep doing what we're doing now."

"That does seem like a good place to start. But it feels hopeless."

"3.1 million isn't the right number anyway. It's quadruple conservative," Dick said. "Remember, we're probably over-estimating our annual expenses and the average future inflation rate. Our Social Security benefit will almost certainly be bigger than we guessed. And, we're intentionally under-estimating the safe withdrawal rate percentage. We used 2.5% instead of 4."

Jane took another sip of wine. "If we need to, we could live on less income too. Like, after the kids are grown, we won't need this big of a house. Can we come up with a number that works but isn't so intimidating?"

"Let's start by seeing what the FV function says."

Scene 41, Sunday, 3/5, Year 4

Jane brought two cups of coffee to the table. Then she looked around the kitchen for the sugar bowl. Finding it, she carried her cup to the counter and stirred in a spoonful.

"I'm afraid to ask," she said. "But what did you learn from the FV function?"

"Thanks for the coffee, Jane," Dick said.

He took a sip. Then he looked at his computer screen.

"The FV function has four inputs," Dick said. "The growth rate, the number of periods (in this case, years), the payment per period which is our combined $20,000 annual 401k and Roth IRA contributions, and the starting amount or Present Value. For the Present Value we'll use the total amount we have in all our retirement accounts right now."

"We know most of those don't we?"

"Yup," Dick replied. "We're looking for a future value in 30 years. We're contributing $20,000 a year. And, we're starting with $80,000 in our retirement accounts."

"Well tell me the bad news."

"The thing is," Dick said, "It's not that bad." He turned the computer around so Jane could see the screen. "Here's a chart of the results using different growth rates."

FV	Rate	Periods	Pmnt	PV
$2,040,643	6.0%	30	20000	80000
$2,498,196	7.0%	30	20000	80000
$3,070,677	8.0%	30	20000	80000
$3,135,321	8.1%	30	20000	80000
$3,787,565	9.0%	30	20000	80000
$4,685,833	10.0%	30	20000	80000

"I see the chart," Jane said. "I guess the 'Rate' column is the Growth Rate. But what does it mean?"

"Think of it as the interest rate. It's the amount the investments would have to grow every year to get to the Future Value number at the end of 30 years."

"Does it apply to both the starting value and to the annual contributions?"

"Yeah," said Dick. "And the Rates in the chart are all within the reasonable range."

"How can that be true? The last FV number is more than twice the first one."

"You're right, of course. But it's just the way compounding works. A 10% growth rate is generally considered about average for the return of the stock market over a long time – like thirty years,"

"If it's average, then sometimes it's worse, right?"

"Right," Dick said. "And sometimes it's higher. But I didn't include higher rates. Anything more than $4,000,000 would be pure gravy."

Dick pointed to the chart. "You can see the 8.1% line is where you get a Future Value of 3.1 million dollars. That has a much higher probability of happening than the 10% average."

Jane paused. She sipped her coffee. Then she said, "Didn't you tell me that when the market is high and interest rates are low like they are now, returns are usually lower than average?"

"Yes, and it's true," Dick said. "That's why I show 6% and 7% lines on the chart. I think we can count on a 6% return as the worst case. With a little luck, we could get 7 or even 8%."

"6% gives us only $2,000,000 in thirty years. I think we should plan on that."

"You're probably right, Dick said. "But don't forget we were quadruple conservative when we calculated our income requirement. Let's take another look at that."

Jane thought for a moment. Then she said, "I don't want to use a lower inflation rate."

"I agree. And I don't want to cut our estimate of expenses. That's our ace in the hole if something goes badly wrong. But I think we can increase our safe withdrawal rate to 4%.

"Yes, I feel better with that. I'm okay with using the 4% safe withdrawal rate. Sally is using 7% for her dividend-based early semi-retirement income. Can't we have our retirement savings invested in things that pay dividends too?"

"We probably can find ETFs that pay dividends," Dick said. "I think that will reduce our risk. It'll for sure reduce the need to sell investments to get the cash for income each year."

"Let's do that then."

"Okay. So, we'll keep the original spending and Social Security estimates. If things work against us, we'll adjust our lifestyle to reduce spending."

"Right. So, how does the math work out."

"$36,000 is our current income budget," Dick said. "With a 3.5% inflation rate that still comes out to about $100,000. Our projected combined Social Security benefits add up to $32,400 per year. 70% of that is 22,700. 100,000 minus 22,700 is 77,300. That's how much we have to cover. We're using a safe withdrawal rate of 4%, so 77,300 divided by .04 is 1,932,500. Rounding up, $2,000,000 is our target number then."

"That's the number on the 6% FV line!"

Dick looked up with a grin. "It's a pretty solid target. It's a good number. We can live well with that. And, we're almost certain to do better."

"Let's celebrate! There's Moose Tracks ice cream in the freezer."

"My favorite. You get the ice cream and I'll make more coffee."

Scene 42, Wednesday, 5/10, Year 4

"That's right Calvin. You've got it now," Lamar said. "Go on and finish your homework. If you have another question, bring it to your mother. It's her turn next."

"Sure, Dad. Thanks." Calvin took his textbook and three-ring binder back to his room.

"So, it's my turn next huh? It's a good thing I'm in a good mood," Sally said. "It's amazing how much difference three hours a week has made. My stress level is a lot lower working forty-five hours instead of forty-eight. Plus, I enjoy engaging with my clients again."

"That's good. I was worried you'd be disappointed when we only put $27,000 in your dividend account to start with."

"No," Sally replied. "I was happy to start cutting my hours so quickly. That was a really good idea you had, Lamar. Thinking of it as a $9,000 investment to produce the $625 per year needed to cut one hour – that made all the difference."

"Speaking of that, the account is almost up to $35,000 now. You'll be able to cut another hour in a week or two."

"Yeah, it should be over $36,000 in two more weeks. But I'm going to wait. I'll delay cutting another hour for at least a couple of weeks."

"Why wait?"

"I'm feeling good about the whole thing now. I want to grow the account faster. Each time the balance increases by $9,000 I could cut another hour. But, If I delay that cut, the extra hour of profit can go straight into the account," Sally said. "I might just stay a whole hour per week behind. I could wait until I increase the balance by $18,000 before I cut one hour. That way there will always be a business surplus. The whole surplus will go in the dividend account. It might not grow much quicker, but speeding it up even a little will feel good."

"It's going to take a long time to reduce your hours down to twenty-four. Can you hold out?"

"I'm pretty sure I can. So far, it's working great. The extra few hours off each week is a relief. Even better is looking forward to getting yet another hour off soon. It might be better this way than getting it all at once. It's like the promise of a new reward each time. A series of small rewards that add up to a big one."

"I love it."

Calvin came in carrying his books again. "Mom," he said. "I need help."

Scene 43, Thursday, 5/11, Year 4

"I'm so glad you could get away to meet me for lunch," Jane said. "I've been looking forward to this all week."

Sally opened the front door of The Perfect Lunch restaurant and motioned for Jane to enter first. As Jane stepped forward, Sally said, "It wasn't a problem. Calvin and Marie are both at school today. And last month I set up formal office hours. My clients know I don't answer the phone between 11:00 am and 2:30 pm."

They approached the reception desk. Jane turned to the maître 'de and said, "It's just the two of us. Could we possibly have the table in the far corner over there?" She pointed to the right rear of the room.

"Let me see. Yes. It's available. Follow me please."

They followed silently until they were seated.

"This table brings back memories," Sally said. "Not all of them good."

"I know. This is where we spilled our guts to each other so many times. I've missed talking things out with you over The Perfect Lunch Special," Jane said with a grin.

"I miss our lunches too. But I don't miss the stress and agonies we shared with each other."

Jane said, "That's the honest-to-God truth, Sally. I can't believe how far we've come since we first heard that Dave Ramsey radio show. Our lives are so different now."

"Different for sure. Less stress. Less arguing with our husbands."

"And you're working from home," Jane said.

At that moment, the server arrived to take their orders. "I'll have The Perfect Lunch Special with a glass of ice water," Jane said.

"I'll have the special too," Sally said, "But please bring me a Diet Coke."

"Certainly ma'am." The server finished writing on his order pad and hurried away.

"Different," Jane said. "We even have a retirement plan that Dick and I believe in. There's a good chance we'll be able to retire early. At least as soon as we're both eligible for Social Security. Sooner if we use your early semi-retirement idea. We'd only have to work to replace our Social Security benefits."

"Wouldn't that be nice?" Sally said. "But what would you do with your time?"

The server returned and set their drinks in front of them. Jane sipped her ice water. She said, "I don't know. But I'd like to be free to choose."

"I get that," Sally said. "I love having more time with the kids. Who knows? When they leave home, I might increase my work hours. If I do, I'll put the extra income in our retirement savings or maybe use some of it for vacations. But it's not like we live in utopia."

"No," Jane agreed. "Dick and I still argue. But not as often and not about money. And with our overall stress levels lower, the arguments just don't seem as bad or as important as they used to be."

"This lunch was a great idea, Jane. Why don't we extend the celebration to include the guys?

Could you and Dick and the twins come over this Sunday? We'll have a cookout."

"That sounds great," Jane said. "Maybe we can talk about early retirement. I wonder if there's a way to make it work?"

Just then the server brought their meals and set them on the table.

Sally raised her glass of Diet Coke and said, "To friendship!"

"And Financial Freedom!"

Part 4: Financial Independence

Scene 44, Sunday, 5/14, Year 4

"The steak is basted and covered, Sally," Lamar said. "How long do you want it to marinate?"

"About an hour, I think. Here, would you carry this tray out to the lounge table? Then you can stay there with Dick. Jane and I will join you in a few minutes."

"Sure. Could you bring us a couple of beers when you come?"

"Of course."

Lamar carried the tray of vegetables, cheese, nuts, and sauces out the back door leading to the patio.

"Is there anything else I can help with?"

"Nah. We're pretty much done with the prep. Would you set that timer for 30 minutes? That's when the casserole needs to go in the oven."

Jane set the timer. "I'll bring the timer when we go outside," she said.

"That's a good idea," Sally said as she washed her hands in the sink. "Are you going to bring up the retire early topic, Jane?"

"For sure," Jane said. "I did some research over the last couple of days. It turns out there's a whole community – a subculture if you will – around the idea of retiring early. It's called the Fire community. F.I.R.E. – it stands for Financial Independence, Retire Early."

"I'm looking forward to hearing about it. Would you like a beer? I'm getting myself one and bringing some out to the boys."

"Do you have a Light?"

"Oh yeah. That's what I'm having too. Here you go,"

They walked out to the patio armed with beer and the timer.

On the patio, four lounge chairs were arranged in a semi-circle around a table. On the far side of the table, a fire blazed in a brick pit. Dick and Lamar sat side by side in the two middle chairs.

Jane took the seat at one end of the arc beside her husband while Sally offered beers to the men.

"Thank you, Sally," Dick said.

"You're welcome, Dick."

"Thanks, my Love," Lamar said.

As she sat next to Lamar, Sally announced, "We'll start grilling in about an hour. And I have to put some things in the oven when the timer goes off in thirty minutes."

Jane reached out and placed the timer on the lounge table.

The two couples chatted amiably for a while. Topics alternated between friends, family, and work.

Finally, Dick looked at Lamar and then at his wife. "Lamar and I noticed you two have been acting a little secretive for several days," he said. "Getting our families together is always fun, but you're cooking up something other than dinner. What is it?"

Sally looked across at Jane. "It's your show," she said.

"Right." Jane was silent for a few seconds. Everyone looked at her expectantly. "I don't know how to start," she said. "I guess I'll just blurt it out." She paused, straightened her back, and said, "I want to see if we can find a way to retire early."

Dick looked into his wife's eyes. "How early. We've been planning to retire in thirty years from now. Are you talking twenty-five years or five?"

Jane gazed into the fire. "I don't know. I guess I want to see what's possible. I mean, five years would be great, but I don't think it's likely." She fell silent again. "In my daydream, we retire when the twins finish college," she said.

"In ten years, the twins will be eighteen. Four years of college would make them twenty-two. So, you're talking about retiring in fourteen or fifteen years?"

"That would be perfect," Jane agreed. "But if it has to be later to make it work it would be okay."

"Where do you fit into this picture, Sally?" Lamar asked.

"Oh, I'm happy with my early semi-retirement plan. But I think we should go along on this ride. Maybe you could retire early too," Sally said.

"Marie is only six," Lamar said. "So, we'd be looking at a twenty-year plan most likely."

"It's better than thirty to thirty-five,"

Dick watched the flames in the fire pit while they talked. Finally, he said, "We wouldn't be eligible for Social Security. And we wouldn't have employer-provided health insurance. We'd have higher expenses and lower guaranteed income. I don't see how it's possible, Jane."

"I don't know if we can do it," Jane said, "but there's a whole sub-culture of people who are doing it. It's called the Fire community (F.I.R.E.). It stands for Financial Independence, Retire Early. Can't we at least look into it?"

"We can look into anything, I guess," Dick said. He looked at Lamar. "What do you think, Lamar?"

Lamar looked first at his wife, then at Jane, and finally turned back to Dick. He said, "You know, three years ago I didn't believe we could get out of debt let alone save for retirement." He paused. "Now... Wow! "I actually think it might be possible to retire early. I don't know how to do it. But I think it might be possible."

"Okay," Dick said. "Let's find out."

Just then the timer buzzed. Sally stood up and said, "It's time to put the casserole in the oven. Who wants another beer while I'm up?"

Lamar said, "Bring another round for Dick and me, please. We have some thinking to do."

Sally headed for the kitchen and Jane followed her.

Scene 45, Saturday, 5/27, Year 4

"You don't know what you're missing, Lamar. This strawberry cheesecake is wonderful," Dick said as he put another forkful in his mouth.

"I'm sure it is," Lamar replied, but if I'm going to eat a dessert, it's got to be chocolate. And, it's hard to beat this double chocolate chip brownie." He took a sip of coffee.

"Well," Dick said, "We're at Panera with pastry and coffee. Our laptops are plugged in and booted up. There is no point in putting it off any longer. It's time to get to work."

Lamar said, "To get started, can you walk me through the process to figure out how much savings you need to retire? It's still a little shaky to me." He lifted a bit of brownie with his fork.

Dick said, "Sure. For Jane and me, it starts with our current income of $68,000 per year. We hope to retire in fifteen years. By then our mortgage will be paid off, the twins should be finished with college, and, of course, we'll stop contributing to our retirement savings when we retire. Our mortgage payments add up to 12,000 a year and we're contributing $20,000 to retirement savings. 68,000 minus 20,000 minus 12,000 = $36,000. That's how much we're living on now, net of those two expenses."

"It's how much you're living on now," Lamar said. "But what about inflation over the next fifteen years? What will you need after inflation?"

"That's the next step," Dick said. "Jane and I agreed to assume a 3.5% inflation rate. That's higher than average and higher than the country's experienced in quite a while. It could turn out a lot worse, but if it does, nothing will work." He punched some keys on his keyboard. "Are you familiar with Excel's FV function?"

"I know about it, but I haven't used it."

"Okay. The FV function is a good way to estimate how any value, or a steady stream of values, will be affected by future growth. It's just an estimate because it assumes a steady growth rate. But it's pretty good, and it's the best available to us." He turned his screen around so Lamar could see it.

"If you look at the cell value detail at the top of the screen, you can see the numbers I entered in the formula."

Lamar looked at Dick's screen. The formula "=-FV(0.035,15,0,36000)" was visible in the cell detail window.

Dick continued, "The first parameter of the formula is the Rate or growth rate. In this case, it's the 3.5% inflation rate we assumed. That's 0.035 when expressed as a decimal. The second parameter is the number of Periods, 15 years. Third, is the Payments per period. We may need this later, but for this calculation it's zero. And finally, the fourth parameter is the present value, PV. This is the beginning value, the $36,000 per year we need now net of the mortgage and retirement savings."

"That makes sense," Lamar said. "Why is there a minus sign at the front of the formula?"

"It's there because the formula gives you a negative number if it's not there. I don't know why. It just does. So, I make it a positive number by putting the minus sign in front. It's a minor irritant."

Lamar said, "The value in the cell is $60,312.56. I guess that's the estimate for what you'll need to live on in fifteen years?"

"That's right," Dick said. "However, I'm going to round it up to $61,000. I'll use 61,000 in the rest of the analysis."

"What about inflation after you retire? In another fifteen years, you might need over 100,000."

Dick turned the computer back so the screen faced him again.

"As a matter of fact, a hundred thousand dollars was exactly the number Jane and I settled on for a retirement in thirty years," Dick said. "But it's a good question. The plan was to deal with inflation after retirement by the way we manage and withdraw from our savings. Do you remember the safe withdrawal rate discussions?"

Lamar said, "I remember. But I also remember that it was based on a 95% probability of not running out of money by the end of a thirty-year retirement. Now you're talking about a forty-five-year retirement. Does that still hold water?"

"Probably not," Dick said. "But let's continue and deal with that later."

"Okay."

"61,000 divided by 4% is 1,500,000. So that's how much money we would need to save to start drawing $61,000 per year in fifteen years at the 4% safe withdrawal rate," Dick said.

"Eh, Dick?"

"What's the matter, Lamar?"

"How can you possibly need only $1,500,000 to last you through a forty-five-year retirement when you figured you needed $1,700,000 for a thirty-year retirement?"

Dick stared at the screen. Then he looked up at the ceiling. "Hmmm...," he said, "and, the thirty-year retirement number assumes we're drawing social security. The forty-five-year retirement doesn't. Implausible."

"Is this the same calculation the FIRE people are using?" Lamar asked.

"Yes, I believe so," Dick replied. "They seem to figure, if bad things happen, they'll just go back to work. I'm beginning to think some of them could find themselves in deep trouble."

"What if we plan on just using dividends? Like Sally's doing."

"Okay. A rough estimate would be $61,000 divided by a 3% dividend yield. That's $2,000,000."

"Sally is getting a 7% dividend yield," Lamar said.

"I know," Dick replied. "Her dividend account is invested in high yielding stocks and ETFs. But it's only a portion of your retirement savings. I'm not willing to risk all of our savings in essentially one asset class. Jane and I agreed that we'll manage our retirement accounts using the asset allocation and rebalancing approach."

"That's where you assign percentages to several uncorrelated investments and buy and sell them to keep the percentages equal, right?"

"Yeah. That's it in a nutshell," Dick said. "We might be able to do better than a 3% yield from the portfolio, but I think 3% is probably a safe assumption."

"So, $2,000,000 then," Lamar said. "Isn't that what you figured you could save after thirty years?"

"Yes, it is," said Dick. "I still have that table of FV functions... Here it is. I'll change the periods from 30 to 15. There. Hmmm... $2,000,000 isn't achievable in fifteen years. Here's the table."

He turned the screen so Lamar could see the chart.

FV	Rate	Periods	Pmnt	PV
$657,244	6.0%	15	20000	80000
$723,303	7.0%	15	20000	80000
$796,816	8.0%	15	20000	80000
$804,608	8.1%	15	20000	80000
$878,617	9.0%	15	20000	80000
$969,629	10.0%	15	20000	80000
$1,183,480	12.0%	15	20000	80000

"I added a 12% growth rate line at the bottom," Dick said, "but even at 12% our retirement savings only grows to $1,200,000. Let's see what happens if we increase our saving rate."

Dick tried entering several different Payment values in his spreadsheet. Finally, he turned the screen around for Lamar to see it again.

"Even at the 12% Growth Rate," he said, "we would have to double our saving rate to $40,000 per year to get close to $2,000,000 in fifteen years. That's just not going to happen. Here's the new chart."

FV	Rate	Periods	Pmnt	PV
$1,122,763	6.0%	15	40000	80000
$1,225,883	7.0%	15	40000	80000
$1,339,858	8.0%	15	40000	80000
$1,351,896	8.1%	15	40000	80000
$1,465,835	9.0%	15	40000	80000
$1,605,079	10.0%	15	40000	80000
$1,929,074	12.0%	15	40000	80000

"That would cut your budget in half, wouldn't it?" Lamar asked.

"More than half," Dick replied. "It would mean 'beans and rice and rice and beans' for a very long time. I don't think we're ready for that. I know I'm not."

"It's not going to work then," Lamar said. "How about an early semi-retirement? Maybe you could start working part-time in fifteen years and delay full retirement until you're eligible for Social Security."

"That's a thought," Dick said. "In fifteen years, the future values in the chart would become the present values for the next fifteen years. Let's see what a second table would look like."

FV	Rate	Periods	Pmnt	PV
$1,575,124	6.0%	15	0	$657,244
$1,995,616	7.0%	15	0	$723,303
$2,527,634	8.0%	15	0	$796,816
$2,588,034	8.1%	15	0	$804,608
$3,200,347	9.0%	15	0	$878,617
$4,050,383	10.0%	15	0	$969,629
$6,477,853	12.0%	15	0	$1,183,480

Dick continued, "If Jane and I just earn enough to live on fifteen years from now, that would be $61,000 adjusted for inflation, we could let our retirement savings grow without adding more to it. In another fifteen years – which puts us at our original thirty-year target date – our savings will grow to more than 1.6 million dollars."

"61,000 is not much less than the 68,000 you earn now."

"That's true," Dick said. "I'll put our current salaries in the formula to see what they would be if they keep up with inflation."

He was quiet as his fingers danced over the keyboard. When they stopped, he said, "If our salaries just keep up with the same 3.5% inflation rate, we'll be earning $113,942 in fifteen years. Call it 114,000. $61,000 is just a little over half of that – 54%.

"So, if you work half-time, that makes your thirty-year retirement work," Lamar said.

"Uh-huh," Dick said. "Our earnings from part-time work would have to continue to keep up with inflation, at least. Although our thirty-year retirement savings target was 1.7 million dollars and this chart predicts less than 1.6 million at the 6% growth rate. I wonder what happens if I add one more year?"

FV	Rate	Periods	Pmnt	PV
$1,669,631	6.0%	16	0	$657,244
$2,135,309	7.0%	16	0	$723,303
$2,729,845	8.0%	16	0	$796,816
$2,797,665	8.1%	16	0	$804,608
$3,488,378	9.0%	16	0	$878,617
$4,455,421	10.0%	16	0	$969,629
$7,255,196	12.0%	16	0	$1,183,480

"Yeah, that does it," he said. "Just under 1.7 million dollars at 6%. So, if the actual growth rate comes in low, we can just continue working part-time for another year or two and It'll still be okay. And another thing, our retirement savings will grow naturally with annual raises. I don't know how much it'll grow. But whatever it is, it'll reduce the time it takes to get to 1.7 million dollars.

"Well, it's a start," Lamar said. "Let's bounce it off the girls."

"Yeah." Dick sipped his coffee. "Yuck! My coffee has assumed room temperature. I'm getting a refill."

"Me too," Lamar said as they both stood up.

Scene 46, Saturday, 5/27, Year 4

"We're done, Mom!" Jacob said, "Can we be excused? We wanna play our video game."

Jane slowly shook her head. "There are so many things wrong with that," she said. "We'll have to deal with them one at a time. First, Jacob, you speak for yourself and John can speak for himself. Try it."

"Can I be excused?" Jacob and John said simultaneously.

"That's one down. Next, when you ask for permission, you say may I be excused, not can I be excused."

"May I be excused?" Jacob said.

"What about you John?"

"May I be excused, too?" asked John

"Two down," said Jane. "Next, you want to play, not wanna play."

"Mom! Everybody says wanna," said Jacob.

"Perhaps," his mother replied, "But you will speak correctly when you speak to me."

"I want to play video games," John said carefully.

Very good, John," You may go."

John shot out of his chair, followed by Jacob.

"Stop!" Dick said. Both boys stopped in their tracks. "John, you may go. Jacob, I don't think you're quite ready yet. Sit back down, please."

Jacob sat and looked down at his plate. When he looked up, he saw his parents both looking at him expectantly. He looked back down. "I want to play my video game," he mumbled.

Dick looked at Jane. "Did you hear something, Jane?"

"Just the wind," she said and continued to stare at Jacob.

Jacob looked up at his mother. "I want to play my video game," he said clearly.

"Okay, go"

He jumped up and ran from the room.

"Well, that was fun," Dick said.

Jane smiled. "It was, wasn't it?"

Dick stood and cleared the dishes from the table. He rinsed them in the sink while Jane wrapped the leftovers and put them in the refrigerator.

"Are you ready to continue our work on retirement planning?" Dick asked.

"Yeah. Now is a good time."

"I may need my computer for the next part of our conversation."

"Okay. Go get it while I wipe the table."

Dick returned a couple of minutes later and set up his laptop. The aroma of brewing coffee filled the kitchen.

He sat across from his wife and asked, "Do you want to ask any questions or should I just pick up where we left off?"

She got up and walked to the coffee pot.

"I guess I want to go over what you said earlier first," she said. "The proposal is that we continue working full-time for fifteen years. During that time, we'll pay off the mortgage, see the twins through college, and keep contributing to our retirement accounts. Then, we'll work part-time for fifteen years. We'll be semi-retired. The mortgage will be paid off, the kids will be out of the house, and we'll stop making retirement account contributions. So, we'll only need to earn a little over half of our full-time salaries. Just enough to cover our living expenses. Is that right?"

"That's it," Dick agreed. "There are a lot of unknowns. But most of them are in our favor."

"Like what? she asked as she poured two cups of coffee.

"That coffee sure smells good," Dick said. "We'll pay off the mortgage before the kids are out of college. That'll free up $12,000 per year while we're still working full-time. Also, we'll probably get raises. They'll automatically increase our 401k contributions. It's possible we could increase them even more."

"How are we going to pay for the twins' college?" Jane asked. "I don't want to saddle them with debt for the rest of their lives."

"Yeah. We haven't talked about that, have we?" Dick responded.

"No. And, it worries me." She set the coffee cups on the table.

"Thanks," Dick said. "Unfortunately, the cost of college fifteen years in the future is very hard to predict. We don't know what kind of school they'll go to or where. We don't know what their interests will be or what their academic strengths and weaknesses will be. We don't know what the tuition will cost." He paused. "We really don't know much at all."

"Can't we make some conservative assumptions like we did when we estimated our retirement expenses?

"We could," Dick agreed. "But the most conservative assumptions would bankrupt us." He sipped his coffee.

"You don't know that," Jane said looking over her steaming cup.

"Okay," Dick said. Let's do a first-level estimate. I heard that tuition to the best state universities is running about $25,000 per year right now. Tack on another $10,000 for other expenses. That's $35,000 for one person - 70,000 for the twins."

"What about inflation?"

"That's a problem. The cost of higher education has been rising faster than overall inflation. They say that it can't keep on doing that, trees don't grow to the sky. But it's been outpacing inflation for decades now. I don't know what number to use. Let's just try 8% to see what happens."

"Are you going to use the FV function?"

"Yup. The PV is $70,000. The twins are eight, so, they'll be eighteen and starting their freshman year in ten years and hopefully graduating in four. But many kids take five years. Let's assume five. Costs will go up during the five years they are enrolled, so I'm going to figure the costs for their fifth year and use that for all five years. That means the Period is 15 years. Using an 8% inflation rate as the Growth Rate gives us an FV of $222,052. That's for one year. For five years it's 1.1 million dollars."

"That's just a lump sum, right? It's a one-time payment, not an on-going need for income," Jane said.

"Yes. But even thinking of it as a lump sum, it's a really big number. Our conservative estimate for the growth of our retirement savings in thirty years is only $2,000,000. And, don't forget, the college expenses will start in just ten years."

"So, what can we do? There must be some way."

"I adjusted the table estimating our retirement savings using a Period of ten years," Dick said. "Look." He turned the screen so Jane could see it.

FV	Rate	Periods	Pmnt	PV
$406,884	6.0%	10	20000	80000
$433,701	7.0%	10	20000	80000
$462,445	8.0%	10	20000	80000
$465,431	8.1%	10	20000	80000
$493,248	9.0%	10	20000	80000
$526,248	10.0%	10	20000	80000
$599,443	12.0%	10	20000	80000

"We could get a little help from the market. If the actual growth rate is higher than 6%, we'll have some cushion we could use to help with college," Dick continued.

Jane said, "Once the mortgage is paid off, we could put the mortgage payment money in a college savings account. Aren't they tax-free?'

"They are," Dick replied. "They're like a Roth, as long as you use the money for education expenses. You contribute after-tax money to 529 accounts and you don't pay taxes on the gains while the money is in the account. When you withdraw the money you only pay taxes on the gains if you use it for something other than education."

He drained his coffee cup and set it on the table.

"What about putting the extra money in our 401k's?" Jane asked. "Isn't there a tax penalty if you withdraw from a retirement account before you are 59? In ten years, you'll only be fifty and I'll be forty-six."

"Technically, the penalty stops when you turn 59 and a half. It's crazy. But that's the rule."

"So that's out, then?"

"No," Dick said. "It's still an option. There's an exception for withdrawing money from an IRA early if you use it to pay for college. You're also allowed to withdraw up to the amount you contributed from a Roth anytime, as long as the money has been in the Roth for at least five years."

"Well, that's something, I guess."

There's a way to use our 401k's too," Dick said. "You remember we're allowed to borrow from them and pay the loan back with interest."

"Yeah, I remember," Jane said. "But we agreed we would never do that."

"Uh-huh. But we could take a loan from our 401k's to help pay for college," Dick said. "It might even be better to do it that way. Even though we have to pay it back with interest, the interest would just increase our retirement account balances. If we had to, we could reduce our regular contributions by the repayment amount. We wouldn't even feel it then. Plus, loans aren't taxable. They aren't official distributions so they don't count as withdrawals."

"If we put all of the extra money in our 401k's, it would reduce our tax bill as we make the contributions too. Wouldn't it?"

"You're right! That would let us contribute even more." Dick said. "Plus, we would have maximum flexibility with the money. If we don't need it for college expenses, it would stay in the retirement account. If we need it for expenses that aren't allowed by the 529 rules, we still wouldn't have to pay taxes on it because it would be a 401k loan."

"I'm starting to like this idea, Dick"

"Me too. Maximum flexibility. Tax-free. No additional accounts to manage. And the possibility of better-than-expected growth."

"Let's do it, Dick. Let's put all the extra money from raises and from paying off the mortgage into our 401k's and take loans from them to help with the college expenses."

"Okay. It's a plan," Dick said. "You know, even while they're in college, it might be better to continue putting our extra money in the 401k's and taking 401k loans for college expenses. That way we would keep getting the tax break for the extra contributions. It would make some of the money we would pay to the IRS go to paying for college instead."

"It's still going to be iffy, isn't it? $220,000 a year is a lot of money," Jane said. "There's no guarantee we can save that much."

"True," said Dick, "We'll need some luck. But we can choose to delay our semi-retirement and use the extra income to refill our retirement accounts. And each of the boys can help by paying some of their own way. They can also apply for scholarships and grants. Even student loans, if necessary."

"Okay. I feel a little better," Jane said. "Do you want more coffee?"

"Please."

Scene 47, Tuesday, 7/4, Year 4

"What a wonderful idea it was to have a Fourth of July party in your backyard," Sally said.

"I'm just glad you could all come," Jane replied.

"Can we see the fireworks from here, Jane?"

"Oh, yes," her friend replied. "Bronson Park is about three blocks over that way. Maybe half a mile. We've had great seats for the Independence Day show ever since they moved it to the park three years ago."

"You can't see the part that's on the ground though."

"No, but we don't have to fight the crowd to get in or out either. And, we have a great view of the 90% of the show that's in the sky."

"No worries about parking either."

"Yup. It's just about perfect," Jane said. "It'll be dark in thirty minutes. The show will start soon after that, I think."

"Let's join the guys on the deck. Right after I pour a glass of Riesling. Would you like one?"

"Certainly. The guys have a cooler of beer out there, but I prefer wine."

"Me too," Sally said. "Beer is okay, but wine is better." Sally smiled and handed Jane a glass of wine and poured another for herself. Then they made their way out to the deck.

Dick and Lamar each had a can of beer in a foam rubber cozy. They sat back in lawn chairs watching the four children running around the backyard.

Red, orange, and purple streaks reflected the sunset from the clouds high overhead.

"What a perfect day," Lamar said. "And here are our lovely ladies who made it so."

"That was a fantastic meal," Dick agreed.

"It was good, wasn't it?" Jane said. "You two did a good job on the grill."

"That was the easy part," Lamar said. "You and Sally did the hard work."

"And great work it was," Dick said.

Sally stared over the deck rail. "What are the kids playing?" she asked.

"We haven't a clue," Lamar said. "We were just wondering about that ourselves."

"Yeah. They seem to be running around mindlessly. But there must be some logic to it."

"Oh well. They're enjoying themselves."

"And, we can see them," Sally said and chuckled. "That's always a good thing."

Quietly, they watched the children for a few minutes. Marie ran to an old oak tree with a tire hanging beside the wide trunk from a chain.

"Push me, Calvin!" Marie called out.

Calvin, Jacob, and John all ran to the tire swing and took turns pushing Marie. Each one gave one push and let another quickly get in position to make the next.

"Wow," said Sally. "What teamwork!"

"We're used to seeing that kind of thing with Jacob and John," Dick said. "But I didn't know it extended to include Calvin and Marie."

"It makes sense though," Jane said. "The twins spend more time with Calvin and Marie than with anyone else, I think. Ken may be a close second."

"Speaking of teamwork," Sally said, "have you two figured out a way to make the early semi-retirement idea work?"

"We have a decent strategy," Dick replied. "It's going to have to be flexible, and we'll need a little luck to fully fund college. But here's the outline. We'll work full-time for at least fifteen more years. We'll pay off the mortgage, increase our retirement savings, and fund college."

Jane said, "When the twins graduate from college and we have at least $700,000 in our retirement accounts, we'll switch to working part-time."

"Will your employers allow that?" asked Lamar.

"Who knows? Even if they would allow it now, they might not in fifteen years."

"But there will be some way to do it, I'm sure of that. Sally's example is an inspiration."

"Yeah," Dick said, "The worst case, I think, is Jane could work part-time, or even stop working altogether while I continue working full-time."

"Maybe I could start a freelance business like you did Sally."

Spot jumped on John playfully. John stepped away from the tree swing and picked up a fallen stick. Spot barked and watched the stick intently.

John reared back and threw the stick across the backyard saying, "Go get it, boy!"

As the big Dalmatian took off after the stick, Marie shouted, "See Spot run!"

Dick chuckled, watching the backyard spectacle. Then he sipped his beer and faced his friends.

"How about you all?" he asked. "Have you made any new plans?"

"I'm happy with my current plan," Sally said. "I'm exploring ways to increase my business income even while I continue gradually reducing my hours. I'm trying to increase the value I deliver to my clients, but that's a business strategy, not a personal finance strategy."

"What about you, Lamar?" Jane asked.

"I'm not in a hurry to retire, at least not now. I like my job. I might feel differently in ten years though. So, I'm focusing on increasing our retirement savings. And on managing the accounts so I can choose to retire early someday if I want to."

"That's smart," said Dick. "Money equals choices, options, and freedom."

"And debt equals stress, conflict, and slavery," Sally said.

"Too bad we didn't understand that ten years ago," Jane said.

"Thank God, we finally learned it," said Dick. "Think about how much worse off we'd be if we hadn't heard Dave Ramsey's radio show three years ago."

"We wouldn't be talking about early retirement, that's for sure!" Jane said.

"How appropriate," Lamar said. "Today is Independence Day and we've finally learned how to live with money."

"It's our Financial Independence Day too," Jane said.

"Look! The fireworks are starting!"

"Beautiful!" Lamar said as the first bombs were bursting in air.

Don't miss out!

Visit the website below and you can sign up to receive emails whenever Mel Clark publishes a new book. There's no charge and no obligation.

https://books2read.com/r/B-A-HCKC-XGBNB

BOOKS 2 READ

Connecting independent readers to independent writers.

About the Author

Mel Clark writes about personal finance, retirement planning, and martial arts.

His blue-collar parents raised him and his two sisters in a wonderful environment for children.

The family, however, was always in debt, always making payments, and never saving.

As a result, Mel is compelled to share hard-won money lessons with working folks. He wants them to know the benefits of saving and investing.

You don't have to be rich to become financially independent.

Mel and his lovely wife Linda live near Virginia's Blue Ridge Parkway. They enjoy ballroom dancing, the occasional camping trip and a silly game called Bananagrams.

Mel is a graduate of the United States Military Academy at West Point and the Darden School of Business at the University of Virginia.

Read more at clearthinkingaboutmoney.blogspot.com/2018/02/sign-up-for-clear-thinking-about-money.html.